A Guide to

CHRISTIAN
CHURCHES

IN THE
MIDDLE EAST

Present-day
Christianity
in the Middle East
and North Africa

Norman A. Horner

**MISSION
FOCUS**

Box 370 • Elkhart, IN 46515-0370

ISBN 1-877736-00-7

Printed in the United States of America

Published by Mission Focus Publications, Box 370, Elkhart, IN 46515-0370.

TABLE OF CONTENTS

Part Two:

THE CHURCHES IN TODAY'S REGION-WIDE TURMOIL:

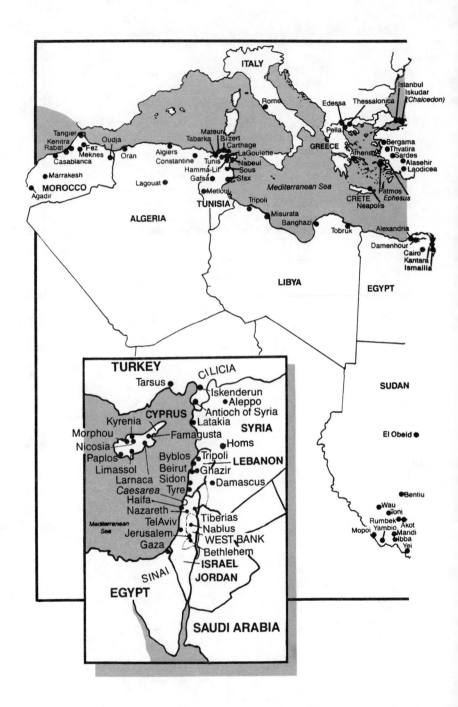

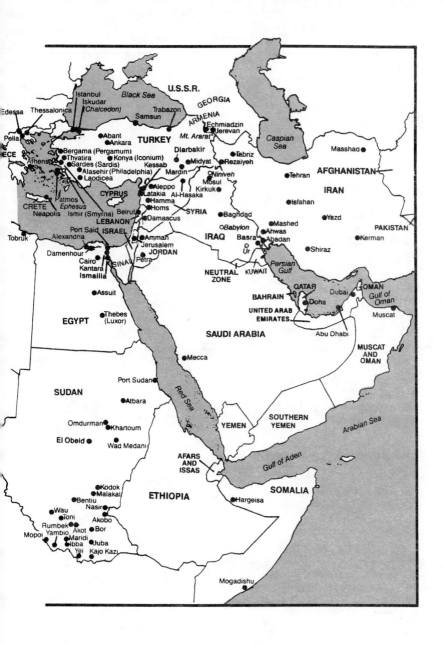

INTRODUCTION

No part of the world has figured more prominently or regularly in Western news reporting over the past fifteen years than the Middle East. The veritable flood of information has focused alternatively on Israel and the Palestinians, the incessant war in Lebanon, the United States hostages, the periodic crises in OPEC, the conflict between Iran and Iraq, and so forth. Ordinary Americans and Europeans may consequently know more than at any other time in history about certain aspects of life in that troubled region. But ignorance about the actual situation of Christians in the Middle East and North Africa remains all but total in most Western circles.

To many Westerners the very existence of thriving Christian communities in the Middle East today comes as a surprise. A common assumption is that Christianity disappeared from that area centuries ago under the impact of Islam. Even the clergy in the West have not been entirely disabused of that erroneous impression. Unless this writer's own experience as a seminarian was unusual, references to the Eastern churches in basic church history courses generally terminate with the record of the celebrated breach between East and West in A.D. 1054. "After that," as one of my more knowledgeable friends once said with tongue in cheek, "everything important happened somewhere between Rome, Italy, and Berkeley, California."

In 1974 I published *Rediscovering Christianity Where It Began: A Survey of Contemporary Churches in the Middle East and Ethiopia* (Beirut: Near East Council of Churches). That booklet of 110 pages was widely appreciated by people in Eastern and Western churches alike. Its reception encouraged me to attempt the present expansion and update, taking into account the political and religious turmoil in the Middle East during the intervening years. In 1983 a Walsh-Price fellowship grant enabled me to undertake necessary travel and research to that end, and I hereby express deep appreciation to the Maryknoll Fathers and Brothers for the generosity of that grant.

A unique feature of my earlier publication was an appendix giving statistical summaries of the approximate total membership and distribution of Christian communities throughout the region. Few others have attempted so comprehensive a count, mainly because there are no reliable written sources for such an undertaking. The predominantly Muslim governments of the area characteristically understate the number of Christians in official publications of their respective countries. To do otherwise would risk a higher proportion of Christian representation in their parliaments and ministries than they are prepared to accept. Church leaders, on the other hand, often

3

tend to exaggerate the size of their constituencies in the Middle East. This leaves the researcher with no choice other than the laborious task of personally consulting as many knowledgeable people as possible in each country, from a wide sampling of all the churches, sifting the evidence, and thereby arriving at more realistic estimates.

Estimates they are—and estimates they will continue to be despite all further efforts to refine them—because accurate statistics simply do not exist. The Eastern churches do not record church membership on an individual basis. That is a more typically Western procedure. One should recognize, moreover, that "membership" in the Eastern churches is primarily a matter of birth and baptism into the Christian communities. Hence the figures I gave in 1974, and their revision in the present writing, represent all who claim to be Christian by birthright or personal choice, whether or not they participate with any regularity in church activities. The same is true, of course, of the way in which the Muslim majority and non-Christian religious minorities in the same region reckon their numerical strength.

Given these limitations of accuracy, one may question the wisdom of getting into this "numbers game" at all. My reason for so doing is to demonstrate graphically to Western readers two facts of which they are not commonly aware: (1) that there **are** Christians throughout the predominantly Muslim Middle East—a remarkably large number and variety of them; and (2) that in the region as a whole the vast majority of them are neither Roman Catholics nor Protestants, but members of the Eastern Orthodox and Oriental (non-Chalcedonian) Orthodox churches, whose presence in the region is not the result of either Protestant or Roman Catholic missionary efforts but dates instead to the earliest centuries of the Christian era.

Ethiopia, included in my earlier publication, does not figure in this revision, and for two reasons: Ethiopia is not properly speaking a part of the Middle East, and in the present political situation in that country the presence of a visiting American researcher would be a disservice to Christians already under suspicion for past associations with the West. Iran, Iraq, and Libya (all of which I visited personally in relation to my earlier study) are here included, but this time on the basis of written or oral sources outside those countries. As of this writing I am unable to get visas to visit them and, in any case, I have no desire to further complicate the lives of people who currently feel the extreme pressures of anti-Western propaganda on the part of their respective governments.

Many of the problems faced by Christians in these regions are centuries old, but several new and baffling issues have arisen within the last ten or fifteen years. Among these are the tragic results of

4

almost continuous warfare in certain of the countries, with consequent massive displacement of peoples and further polarization of ideologies. There has also been a radical change in the attitudes of certain governments with respect to their Christian minorities, prompted in part by the region-wide emergence of Islamic fundamentalism. Continuing Israeli intransigence, supported by Western nations with whom some Middle Eastern Christians have historic relationships, is another divisive factor of serious proportions. All of this conditions the ways in which the Christian communities relate to one another and to their wider political and religious environment.

Massive emigration has considerably eroded the strength of Christianity in some parts of the region during the last decade or longer. But, while that fact should not be denied or minimized, not all such emigrations have taken people overseas. Some of them have merely meant a redistribution, temporary or permanent, within the region itself, thus bringing an increase in Christian numbers and vitality to other parts of the same area. This, along with the relative stability of the Christian populations in Syria, Egypt, Jordan, and elsewhere, means that the overall numerical strength of Christians in the region as a whole is greater than I found it in 1974. This is contrary to my expectation when I undertook the present study, and I rejoice in it. There are actually many more Christians in the Middle East than there were fifteen years ago, and this despite the fact that steady emigration from Jerusalem, the Israeli-occupied West Bank, and Turkey still threatens to reduce those once lively centers of Christian activity to mere ecclesiastical museums.

The following pages briefly describe the origins of the churches throughout the Middle East and the North African Maghrib (the Arab West), their present-day character and distribution, their involvement in the current political and religious environment, and their relationships with the Muslim majority. This material in an expanded format was presented as the William T. and Virginia H. Ingram Lectures at Memphis Theological Seminary of the Cumberland Presbyterian Church in March 1986.

THE CHURCHES OF THE MIDDLE EAST:
Origins and Present Distributions

The breach between Eastern and Western Christianity has kept the churches of the two hemispheres in virtual isolation from one another for the past nine hundred years. This is somewhat less true since 1948, when some of the Eastern churches began their associations with the then newly organized World Council of Churches, and especially since 1961 when others followed the Russian Orthodox Church into Council membership. Yet this legacy of mutual isolation throughout nearly half the total span of Christian history to date accounts in large measure for the slow progress of interchurch fellowship even today. When the Ecumenical Patriarch Athenagoras and Pope Paul VI finally met in Jerusalem in January 1963 to abrogate the anathemas pronounced in the eleventh century, the Patriarch is credited with having made a most interesting comment. A brash young news reporter encountered him on the path one day and said: "Your Holiness, I have to write a very brief article about your meeting. Would you tell me in just one or two sentences what it is that separates you from the Roman Pope?" Athenagoras pulled himself up to the impressive height of his striking physique and replied, "What separates us is nine centuries of separation."

More than eight million Christians now live in the area from western Turkey to eastern Iran, and from northern Syria to southern Sudan. Except for Cyprus they are everywhere minorities within their respective countries, and in some of those countries very tiny minorities indeed, but they are everywhere vigorous and indomitable minorities.

The diversity of Christian churches in the Middle East is as great as in any other part of the world and much greater than in most other regions. Virtually the entire spectrum of worldwide Christianity is represented. There are Eastern (Byzantine) and Oriental (non-Chalcedonian) Orthodox churches, Catholics of Latin and Oriental rites, the Assyrian (Nestorian) Church of the East, Anglicans, various Protestant denominations, and a large number of sectarian groups. Some of these churches have been there from earliest Christian times. Others emerged in the course of theological and political disputes in early centuries. Some are the result of proselytizing zeal at various periods including the nineteenth and twentieth centuries.

That the world's oldest churches are still to be found in the Middle East is unquestionable. Churches established in apostolic times have continued there in one form or another ever since, and in their own traditions a number of them claim very specific apostolic founders: James in Jerusalem, Peter and Paul in Antioch (as well as in Rome), Thomas in Babylonia (and as far as India), Mark in Alexandria, Barnabas in Cyprus, and so forth. Pious traditions of this kind are not historically verifiable, but they are persistent among people who have honored them for long centuries and they are not to be scorned. Of more historic certainty, five patriarchates or major Christian centers emerged within the Roman Empire in the early centuries of the Christian era: Rome, Constantinople, Alexandria, Antioch, and Jerusalem—all of them except Rome in the Middle East. Farther east, in the regions then under Persian domination, the most important Christian centers were at Seleucia-Ctesiphon (near modern Baghdad) and Echmiadzin (today in Soviet Armenia just north of the Iranian border). The contemporary Eastern churches are related to those ancient patriarchates, and the present divisions among them are the result of political and theological controversies that have marked the history of the patriarchates themselves.

It is a more elusive and probably futile quest to determine which among the churches in the Middle East today are the oldest. That decision rests, I suppose, upon rather arbitrary and subjective determinants. In the several major divisions that occurred, beginning at the Council of Ephesus in A.D. 431, which of the resulting churches are the "separatists" and which may be properly designated the "continuing church?" The answers of the people who live in the area will depend very largely upon their personal allegiances, because each community claims to have preserved the truth in its orthodox purity. Nevertheless the non-Chalcedonian Orthodox churches (Armenian, Coptic, and Syrian) claim that they alone have maintained the character of truly "national" churches from the beginning. In contrast to the Eastern Orthodox they steadfastly resisted the cultural and linguistic influences of both Rome and Constantinople on their respective homelands, and they insist that Islam became predominant in this once widely Christianized area because the Christian churches were so divided by culturally alienating influences from those capital cities of Old and New Rome.

I. Eastern (Chalcedonian) Orthodox Churches

Four Eastern Orthodox Patriarchates and one national Archbishopric are in the Middle East today: Jerusalem, Antioch (now centered in Damascus), Alexandria, Constantinople (now Istanbul), and the Church of Cyprus. They all belong to the Byzantine tradition, that great branch of Orthodoxy which also includes ten other autocephalous or self-governing churches (Russia, Romania, Serbia, Greece, Bulgaria, Georgia, Czechoslovakia, Poland, Albania, and Sinai). To call the five that are found in the Middle East "Greek Orthodox," as is often done, is merely to identify them with the Byzantine mainstream and not to suggest that their people are all Greeks either ethnically or linguistically. Those of the Antioch and Jerusalem Patriarchates, for example, are Arabs who use an Arabic liturgy. Constantinople, the capital of Byzantium, was long called "New Rome," and hence the common Arabic designation of Christians related to the Byzantine patriarchates in the Middle East is in English translation "Roman Orthodox."

Eastern Orthodox churches are different from the Oriental (non-Chalcedonian) Orthodox in two important respects. First, in their theology, the Eastern Orthodox recognize the authority of seven ecumenical councils held between the fourth and eighth centuries: Nicea (325), Constantinople (381), Ephesus (431), Chalcedon (451), Constantinople II (553), Constantinople III (680), and Nicea II (787). The word "ecumenical" in its root meaning is "the inhabited world." As used with reference to those councils it means the Christian world of those centuries. At the fourth council (Chalcedon, 451) a major division occurred over the relationship between the two natures, human and divine, in the person of Christ. It is the continuing insistence of the Eastern Orthodox upon the Christological formula adopted at that council[1] which distinguishes them from the large Eastern churches known as Oriental or "non-Chalcedonian" Orthodox (Syrian, Coptic, and Armenian). Second, in their polity, the Eastern Orthodox recognize the Patriarch of Constantinople as "Ecumenical Patriarch," first among equals. This is a largely honorary primacy, quite different from the Roman Catholic concept of papal authority, because each of the churches in this Eastern Orthodox group is entirely self governing.

8

A. *The Patriarchate of Jerusalem*

As other great Christian centers developed in both East and West during the early centuries, the "Mother Church" in Jerusalem was rapidly overshadowed by her "daughter churches." Yet Jerusalem, the place where Christian history began, where Jesus died and rose again, the center from which the first apostles took the gospel into other parts of the world, never lost its centrality in the hearts of Christian people. At the Council of Chalcedon in 451 the primate of Jerusalem was given a place of honor next after that of Alexandria and Antioch, and so it is to this day even though the number of people in this patriarchate has never been large enough to make it a major power in the Orthodox world.

The members of this church today nevertheless constitute more than half the total Christian population of the Israeli-occupied West Bank and in Jordan. Most of them are Arabs, as are the parish priests, celebrating the Orthodox liturgy in Arabic. However, the entire hierarchy (patriarch, bishops, and the Brotherhood of the Holy Sepulchre) are Greeks. This is a vestige of historical circumstances that long ago gave the Greek-speaking Orthodox a major responsibility in the protection of the holy places. The Greek hierarchy jealously guards that prerogative, but it is presently under considerable criticism from both priests and laity. With the rise of Arab nationalism it seems increasingly anachronistic and in time is likely to change, just as the Antioch Patriarchate has been able to insist on an Arab hierarchy since 1899.

The holy places in and around Jerusalem are a focal point of sacred memory for all Christians in the world, most especially for those of the Eastern churches. Unfortunately the supervision of those holy places, notably the Church of the Holy Sepulchre itself, has long been a source of contention among the several Christian communities represented in the city and environs. The reasons for such disputes are complex and beyond the purview of this brief study to discuss, but the resulting animosities are a scandalous perversion of the Christian spirit. The much larger question of properly supervising the places sacred to all three monotheistic faiths is a matter of utmost importance to the restoration of peace in the Middle East today.

Diodoros, the present Patriarch of Jerusalem, was formerly archbishop in Jordan. Fifteen archbishops and metropolitans comprise the hierarchy. The offices of many are now merely titular, preserving the names of the actual dioceses of early centuries: Caesarea, Petra, Nazareth, Pella, Neapolis, Gaza, Lydda, Kyriakoupolis, Sebasteia, Jordan, Eleutheroupolis, Hierapolis, and Diocaesarea. There is a colony of monks at the Mar Saba Monastery in addition to the larger Brotherhood of the Holy Sepulchre. The monastic community of the renowned St. Catherine Monastery in Sinai is in its own right an autonomous archdiocese linked closely with the Patriarchate of Jerusalem.

The Church of Russia once had important institutions in Jerusalem, largely because of its many pilgrims to the Holy Land. The Russians still have a prominent church building in Jerusalem and a chapel in the Garden of Gethsemane. They also continue a limited amount of welfare work in the area. However, their representation in personnel now consists exclusively of a few priests and nuns. The nuns have convents in both Jerusalem and Bethany, and they receive some Arab girls as novices. The Synod of Russian Orthodox Bishops Outside Russia, a vigorously anti-communist group in separation from the Moscow Patriarchate, now maintains a building in Jerusalem near the Church of the Holy Sepulchre.

B. The Patriarchate of Antioch

Antioch of Syria, where our forebears in the faith were first called Christians (see Acts 11:26) was a major center of theological and liturgical development for many centuries. At the Council of Chalcedon in A.D. 451, Antioch was ranked third in dignity among the Eastern Orthodox patriarchates, after Constantinople and Alexandria, reflecting the relative importance of those three centers in the early church. Today Antioch is no longer in Syria at all, and only very small Christian communities are to be found there. It is an almost solidly Muslim town, called Antakya, in modern Turkey where scattered ruins dimly attest its importance to early Christendom.

Yet the name of Antioch is fixed in the memory and tradition of all Eastern Christians. Over the centuries a number of political and theological disagreements have so divided the once-united patriarchate that there are now five primates of as many different churches who all use the title "Patriarch of Antioch and All the East": Eastern Orthodox, Melkite (Greek Catholic), Syrian Orthodox, Syrian Catholic, and Maronite. None of their sees is any longer in Antioch itself, political contingencies and shifting populations having forced their removal from place to place since the time of the Crusades. Damascus is now the center for the first three named above. The other two reside in or near Beirut.

The Eastern Orthodox Patriarchate of Antioch is today by far the largest, liveliest, and most progressive segment of Eastern Orthodoxy in the Middle East. Its sister patriarchates of Constantinople and Alexandria have lost most of the former Greek populations on which they depended, and Jerusalem's Arab constituency remains dominated by a highly traditional Greek hierarchy.

Arab leadership and a solidly Arab membership are indeed the explanation for the Antioch Patriarchate's continuing development and contribution to the region in modern times. With help from the Church of Russia, Antioch was able to elect its first Arab patriarch in 1899, and since that time it has remained free of foreign control. In all respects—language, culture, politico-social involvements—it is a self-conscious part of the Arab world and, as such, the diverse political ideologies of that troubled society are all represented within the church and have sometimes threatened its internal cohesion.

Identity with Arab culture has enabled this church to provide significant leadership to the modern Arab awakening, and to coexist more creatively with the Muslim majority than is the case with most other churches in the area. Lacking strong ties with the West, such as those that characterize Catholic and Protestant groups in the region, and being relatively free from the violent encounters with Muslim governments that have been the historic experience of both Armenian and Syrian Orthodox, the Eastern Orthodox Patriarchate of Antioch long ago made its sometimes uneasy but lasting peace with Islam. There is all too little Christian-Muslim dialogue of any formal kind anywhere in the Arab East, but such as there is enjoys the participation of this Antioch Patriarchate.

This patriarchate now has a total of ten dioceses in the region. Five are in Syria (Aleppo, Latakia, Hamma, Homs, and Akkar), together comprising by far the largest Christian community in that country. Another four are in Lebanon (Beirut, Mt. Lebanon, Tripoli, and Zahle-Baalbek) where its twenty percent of the total Christian population is exceeded by only one other church, the Maronite Catholics. Along with its numerous parishes and some seventeen small monasteries, this Antioch Patriarchate maintains twenty-five primary schools in Syria and Lebanon, a dozen secondary schools, and a hospital (in Beirut). The remaining diocese, Baghdad, is served by a bishop who resides in Kuwait but is responsible as well for the relatively small Eastern Orthodox communities in Iraq, Iran, and the Arabian Gulf States. A very large diaspora, perhaps as many as a million in total, is in Europe, North America (three bishops), South America (five bishops), and Austral-Asia. The importance of this diaspora is evident, not only to the financial support of work throughout the patriarchate but also to inter-church relationships in the West. The present patriarch, Ignatius IV Hazim, is a distinguished theologian and an internationally recognized leader in the ecumenical movement. Currently a member of the World Council of Churches Central Committee, he was for several years co-chairman of the World Student Christian Federation. He continues to serve as one of the three presidents of the Middle East Council of Churches (MECC), a post to which he was elected at the organizational meeting of that council in 1974, three years before he became Patriarch of Antioch.

Ignatius IV has long championed the most progressive developments in the patriarchate. As a young priest in 1942, he helped to launch the Orthodox Youth Movement (OYM) for intellectual and spiritual renewal among university students in Lebanon and Syria. In 1953 the OYM took leadership in the formation of SYNDESMOS, the worldwide and pan-Orthodox youth organization. It is also credited with having spearheaded a revival of monasticism that had lost the vitality and creativity of earlier centuries. That revival continues to bring highly educated young men and women to commitment in monastic living at two Lebanese centers in particular: Deir Mar Yakoub (for women) near Tripoli, and Deir al-Harf (for men) near Beirut. There are currently twenty-one nuns at the former and eight monks at the latter. Both centers nurture spirituality, iconography, and liturgical renewal in ways that are felt throughout the church.

But perhaps the most remarkable achievement of the present patriarch is the university-level Theological Institute of St. John of Damascus near Tripoli, Lebanon. During the late 1960s and early 1970s, when Hazim was the superior at Balamand Monastery and responsible for the training of seminarians housed there, he determined to recapture the educational prestige the Antioch Patriarchate had enjoyed in early centuries. Almost single-handedly he pressed that cause among his colleagues in the hierarchy. He solicited aid from the Antiochene dioceses in North America and from the World Council of Churches to finance an ambitious building program. The result is a striking complex of buildings adjacent to the ancient Balamand Monastery and overlooking Tripoli harbor.

This Theological Institute got underway with less than a dozen students in the mid-1970s, just as the civil war in Lebanon began to disrupt all such activities. But throughout the next years of intermittent violence in the country the student body continued, even grew in numbers, although classes were forced to meet at different locations from time to time. Visiting professors from the Church of Greece were brought in to supplement the faculty in certain areas. Today the St. John of Damascus Institute has sixty students. Most of them are Syrians and Lebanese, but there continue to be a few Palestinians from the Jerusalem Patriarchate where there is no adequate training for the Arabic-speaking clergy.

"This Institute makes it entirely unnecessary for us to send students to Athens, Salonica, or Moscow as we had to do earlier," Patriarch Ignatius said to this writer with evident satisfaction. "And it enables us to help educate the clergy of a sister patriarchate as well." A diligent young librarian is now working to rebuild the collection of books and ancient manuscripts, only a small part of which has been recovered from the theft and destruction of the war years, and to classify new acquisitions.

The war in Lebanon and turmoil throughout the region as a whole have brought suffering to the people of this Antioch Patriarchate no less than to other Christian communities. But although both liberal and conservative political ideologies are voiced within their church, they are not tempted by the willingness of Maronite extremists to further divide Lebanon if need be to create a state composed entirely of Christians. Neither are they prepared to collaborate in any way with Israel at the expense of the Palestinians. They have long resented Maronite domination in Lebanon's affairs and would readily opt for a secular state rather than the confessional system on which that country's government has been based since independence in 1943. To this writer's inquiry about how the almost continual warfare since 1975 has affected the aspirations of his people, one of the church's prominent bishops replied: "It has made us more 'eschatological.' We no longer think in terms of human power, but only of God's power and God's ultimate victory."

C. The Patriarchate of Alexandria

Alexandria, once very large and powerful, is now least in size among the Eastern Orthodox patriarchates of the Middle East. The first massive reduction began in the latter part of the fifth century when the vast majority of Egyptian Christians rejected the Council of Chalcedon. From that time onward the non-Chalcedonian Coptic Orthodox Church (see description in Section III, below) became the predominant Patriarchate of Alexandria, leaving the Eastern Orthodox patriarchate to a primarily Greek-speaking minority. For centuries thereafter, that minority continued to be substantial and influential. Even in 1920 there were still about 250,000 Greeks in Egypt and North Africa, but their number steadily decreased thereafter. Since 1958 a more precipitous emigration of the Greek population from the region has reduced the membership of this patriarchate to a small fraction of its earlier strength.

The present Pope and Patriarch of Alexandria and All Africa nevertheless retains title to his historic prestige in the Eastern Orthodox family of churches, next in dignity to the Patriarch of Constantinople. The church he administers now has four dioceses in Egypt: Alexandria (including Cairo), Hermopolis (Tanta), Leontopolis (Ismal'ilia), and Pelusium (Port Said and Kantara). There are fifty-five parish churches in Egypt, with an active membership of about seven thousand and a total constituency of about twice that number. Less than half are native Egyptians. The Archdiocese of Nubia (Sudan and upper Egypt) has another eighteen hundred members. A total of no more than two thousand Greek expatriates belong to the Archdiocese of Carthage (Tunisia, Algeria, Libya, and Morocco).

Despite its numerically weakened condition in Egypt and North Africa, this patriarchate maintains some ten primary-secondary schools and several orphanages, clinics, and homes for the aged. One of its truly great institutions is the Greek Orthodox Library in Alexandria. The famous Christian library of early centuries in that city was completely destroyed long ago, but this one may be regarded as its lineal descendent. Over thirty thousand books and manuscripts, the oldest of them dating to the ninth century, are carefully catalogued and handsomely displayed. This library is an important tool for historical and ecumenical research.

The eight other dioceses of the Alexandria Patriarchate are in cities and nations outside the limits of this study: Johannesburg and Praetoria, Capetown, Zimbabwe, Central Africa (Zaire), Accra and West Africa, Axum (Ethiopia), and Irinopolis (East Africa). The local churches in those vast areas have been established for the most part to serve the expatriate Greek-speaking population, but indigenous African members are in some of them. Indeed the liveliest hope for the future of this patriarchate lies with a completely indigenous and growing movement among Black Africans in Kenya and Uganda. It began in the 1920s, was formally recognized by the Patriarch of Alexandria in 1946 and constituted as the Archdiocese of Irinopolis in 1958. A Greek archbishop and three African bishops now comprise the hierarchy. Total communicant membership is estimated at ninety thousand—more than all other segments of the patriarchate combined! There is little expectation that people of Greek origin will return in numbers to the Arabic-speaking regions of North Africa. Hence the membership of this patriarchate can grow only by natural increase in the families that remain there and by missionary outreach into other parts of the continent. But if this movement in Kenya and Uganda continues to flourish, and if there are greater efforts to expand among indigenous Africans elsewhere on the continent, the Alexandria Patriarchate may yet regain a position of strength in Eastern Orthodoxy.

D. *The Patriarchate of Constantinople*

From the early part of the fourth century Constantinople (now Istanbul) was known as "New Rome." The Council of Chalcedon accorded to its patriarch a rank second in prestige only to that of the Roman pontiff. Constantinople was capital of the Eastern Roman Empire, and long after the decline of that empire it remained the focal center of Eastern Orthodoxy. Ever since the eleventh-century breach between Eastern and Western churches, those of the Eastern Orthodox family have called the Patriarch of Constantinople "the Ecumenical Patriarch."

During the centuries of Ottoman rule, and up to the time Turkey became a secular state after the first world war, this patriarch was obliged to assume a different kind of authority than the churches had ever intended. The Ottomans, in their "millet" system for the rule of religious minorities, regarded him as not only spiritual leader of the Greek Orthodox Church but also civil head of the entire Orthodox millet. Thus he was no longer merely first in dignity among the Orthodox patriarchs of the Middle East, but those in Alexandria, Antioch, and Jerusalem were made subordinate to him. This was in flagrant violation of the Orthodox principle of self-governing churches. It also brought a great deal of distress to the Constantinople Patriarchate itself, because the election of each new patriarch became an occasion for bribery, political intrigue, and other corruption.

With the emergence of the new Turkish state in the 1920s, that particular problem was solved, but in other ways the patriarch's position became even more difficult. In the mind of the Turkish authorities he was the unwelcome symbol of Greece and everything Greek. Opposition rose to a crescendo at every military or political confrontation between Turkey and Greece. In 1959 nearly three-fourths of all the Greek Orthodox parish churches in Istanbul and the surrounding areas were destroyed or badly damaged by angry mobs. The Turkish-Greek dispute over Cyprus has kept the patriarch's situation in very delicate balance ever since.

The name of Athenagoras I, Patriarch of Constantinople until his death in July 1972, became a household word among Christians everywhere because of his significant leadership in the worldwide ecumenical cause. His successor and the present Ecumenical Patriarch is Demetrius I, a man of deep pastoral concerns and greatly respected by the Greek population. Demetrius lacks the worldwide experience of his predecessor, however, and is not well known outside Greek Orthodox circles. Neither has he been able thus far to initiate a meaningful dialogue with the Turkish government.

The patriarchate over which Demetrius rules was once larger in the Middle East itself than the other three Eastern Orthodox patriarchates. That is no longer the case. It is now smaller than any of the others except Alexandria. Over the last sixty years Christians of all confessions have emigrated from Turkey, and the Greek Orthodox have lost proportionately more than most of the others. Since 1964 alone, their total membership has declined from an estimated forty-five thousand to no more than seven thousand. Yet they continue to maintain a structure of four dioceses in that country: Chalcedon, Derkos, Prinkipos, and Imbos-Tenedos. Within those dioceses are about fifty parish churches, more than twenty primary and secondary schools, an orphanage, a dispensary, and a small home for the aged.

Halki, the theological school of the Constantinople Patriarchate, is located on Heybeli Island near Istanbul. It was until recently a major center for the training of Orthodox clergy from many parts of the world, and parish priests of this patriarchate have a higher level of education than is the case elsewhere in the Middle East. But in 1972 a new Turkish law limiting higher education to government-controlled institutions made it impossible for this seminary to continue except as a secondary school.

Despite its small and still declining membership in the Middle East proper, the Patriarchate of Constantinople has a constituency in other parts of the world of about three million Eastern Orthodox Christians: ultimate ecclesiastical authority over the Church of Crete, four archbishoprics in the Dodecanese (Aegean Islands), the exarchate of Patmos, the monastic state of Mt. Athos in Greece, the Orthodox Church of Finland, and the very large Greek Orthodox diaspora in North and South America, Australia, New Zealand, Great Britain, France, Belgium, Sweden, Germany, and Austria.

E. The Church of Cyprus

Cyprus, with a total population of only 640,000, is nevertheless an important link in the chain of Eastern Orthodoxy. There may be some question about classifying Cyprus as a part of the Middle East because of the overwhelming Greek-Cypriot majority in its population, but the Island's geographical location—well to the east of Asia Minor—and its large Turkish minority justify its inclusion in this survey. The small republic's involvement in the politico-religious affairs of the region further suggests that it must not be omitted.

The Eastern Orthodox Church of Cyprus has a fascinating history. Tradition traces its origins to the middle of the first Christian century, when the Roman governor of the island was converted to Christianity under the ministry of the apostles Paul and Barnabas (see Acts 13). Barnabas, himself a Cypriot, is the church's patron saint and is still memorialized by his fellow countrymen in icons, monasteries, the names of church and school buildings, and in the daily liturgy.

The Church of Cyprus was ruled from Antioch in early centuries, but has been recognized as entirely autocephalous since the Council of Ephesus in A.D. 431. Following the discovery in Cyprus of the relics of St. Barnabas in 478, the church's autonomy was again confirmed by the Byzantine Emperor Zeno. Zeno further authorized the Archbishop of Cyprus, alone among church primates, to wear a cape of imperial purple, to carry an imperial sceptre, and to sign his documents in red ink.

Cyprus was the first Orthodox land to be conquered by the Crusaders, in 1191, and for nearly four centuries thereafter it was dominated by the Latin Church, especially the Venetians. The Ottoman occupation in 1571 restored authority to the Church of Cyprus. But the Ottomans also introduced the settlement of a large Turkish colony on the island, thus laying the foundations of an ethnic problem that has vexed the island's domestic and international relationships ever since.

In 1660 the archbishop was recognized by the Ottomans as ethnarch, temporal as well as religious head of his Greek-speaking "nation," subject of course to the final authority of the Ottoman sultan. (The much later election of Archbishop Makarios III as both head of the church and president of the new republic from 1960 to 1977 was therefore not without precedent.)[2] But during the British rule from 1878 to 1959 the church's role as a political force was severely curbed. It was during this British rule that the popularity of

17

the ENOSIS (union-with-Greece) movement flourished.

The Church of Cyprus continues to be the national focus of the Greek-Cypriot community, and the percentage of Christians in the total population is much higher than in any other country of the Middle East. Moreover, this church has been remarkably successful in protecting its membership from the proselytizing activities of others through the centuries. In Cyprus the people are legally free to change their ecclesiastical allegiance, but very few have done so in modern times. About ninety-eight percent of all Christians in the country still belong solidly to this one church.

Virtually all aspects of social and cultural life on the island have been conditioned by the church. Yet the role of the hierarchy as Ethnarchic Council ended with the independence of Cyprus in 1960. This, and the secularization that affects Cyprus along with the rest of the modern world, have undoubtedly eroded the church's former influence to some extent. Dr. Benedict Englezakis, a lay theologian at the archbishopric, wrote: "Like all beloved old people, the church can sometimes be gossiped about or laughed at, but she still knows how to reply in kind. And though the young generation of our pluralist society seems anxious to offer her a comfortable retirement, she is not going to give in. She is already taking care of her appearance and will soon find other ways of becoming attractive to the young."[3]

Chrysostomos I, the former Bishop of Paphos, was elected Archbishop of Nova Justinia and All Cyprus upon the death of Makarios in 1977. The archbishopric is housed in a building of striking beauty within the old city walls of Nicosia. In addition to Nicosia there are five other dioceses of the church: Paphos, Kition (Larnaca), Kyrenia, Limassol, and Morphou. Some seven hundred ordained priests serve this church of 480,000 members.

The Theological Seminary of St. Barnabas was established in 1950. It is located in a suburb of Nicosia and now has about fifty students. Until recently the course was only two years beyond high school, but the seminary is in process of expanding its curriculum to the level of a theological college. Those who teach religion in the schools of either church or state are generally laymen, and most of them have completed theological studies at the universities of Athens or Thessalonica. There is as yet no university or college of liberal arts in Cyprus.

Monasteries still play an important role in the life of this church. In 1960, at the beginning of national independence, the total wealth of the church and its monasteries was reported to be in excess of 150 million pounds sterling, along with 176,000 acres of farm land—a heritage from Ottoman times when Christians donated their property to the church to avoid having it confiscated by the government.[4] The largest monastery is Kykko, high in the Troodos mountains. Six monks are currently in residence there, and fourteen others reside at that monastery's priory in Nicosia. Kykko community is involved in a number of agricultural and business enterprises, and contributes to the life of the country in a variety of ways. Stavrovouni and Trooditissa are other well known male monastic centers, and there are several women's convents.

The church conducts catechetical schools in every parish and village. It sponsors women's unions, associations of scholars, and five welfare projects. A church press publishes new books annually, along with a monthly periodical called *Apostle Barnabas*, specialized journals for the priests, and a bi-monthly newspaper for teenagers. The Archbishop Makarios III Foundation, housed at the archbishopric in Nicosia, has a celebrated collection of icons, paintings, Cypriot antiquities, and folk art. The largest library in the country, with manuscripts, historical archives, and about fifty thousand volumes of classical, Byzantine, and Cypriot studies is part of this Foundation. In 1979 the Foundation provided the country with a new pediatric hospital and institute on thalassemia, a hereditary anemia prevalent in countries bordering the Mediterranean.

The Church of Cyprus is virtually limited to the boundaries of its small nation. But its vitality is felt in distant places. In recent years it has greatly encouraged the indigenous movement to Orthodoxy in East Africa. These new Eastern Orthodox Christians, mostly in Kenya and Uganda, belong administratively to the Patriarchate of Alexandria. But much of the help they have received, including funds to build a seminary and vocational school in Nairobi, are from the Church of Cyprus. The seminary opened in January 1982 with thirty-two students in the first class. The director and his associate are both Greeks from the Alexandria Patriarchate.[5]

II. The Assyrian ("Nestorian")
Church of the East

Traditions of the ancient Church of the East trace its origins to Thomas the Apostle[6], Thaddeus (Addai) one of the Seventy Disciples (Luke 10:1,17), and Mari, a first-century Persian Christian. The patriarchs of this church came to be called "occupants of the throne of Mar Addai and Mar Mari." Whatever weight may be given to those particular traditions, the Christian community that now calls itself the Assyrian Church of the East had very early origins. In addition to "Church of the East," its earliest designation, five names have been variously used throughout history in reference to this particular branch of Christendom: East Syrian, Church of Persia, Chaldean, Nestorian, and Assyrian.

The term "East Syrian" as applied to these people does not mean inhabitants of Syria but rather their use of the Syriac (Aramaic) language, and their early associations with Antioch. Among the five churches that use Syriac in their respective liturgies (Syrian Orthodox, Maronite, Syrian Catholic, Chaldean Catholic, and Assyrian Church of the East), only the last two named use the Eastern dialect of that language, but all five stem from the traditions of the once undivided Patriarchate of Antioch. Moreover, the Syrian Orthodox ("West Syrians") and the Assyrian Church of the East ("East Syrians") have such commonality of origins and early history that even the Christological dispute of the fifth century, in which the two churches were and still are at opposite poles, was not strong enough to completely destroy their sense of being in fact one people.

The Church of the East came to be called "the Church of Persia" when, in the sixth century, the Persians' toleration of Christians living within their orbit was conditional upon complete independence of the Antioch Patriarchate. Thus one more instance of political exploitation of theological differences throughout history! Persia and New Rome were enemies, and Antioch was within the Roman realm. The Catholicos (supreme bishop) of the East had his see at Seleucia-Ctesiphon, a few miles south of modern Baghdad, then a part of the Persian Empire and the most important Christian center outside Roman territory. The jurisdiction of this catholicosate over some twenty-five bishoprics had existed for more than two centuries (since A.D. 280) under the ultimate authority of Antioch. But relationships had become increasingly tenuous, and the Synod of Seleucia in A.D. 499 finally ended any further dependence. The Church of Persia then became entirely autocephalous.

This church was enlarged in numbers by many thousands of refugees from the Western regions. It enjoyed a remarkable missionary expansion during the following seven centuries, reaching as far as India and China. This energetic movement began in the sixth century, reached its peak in the eighth, and continued up to the thirteenth. The Persian cross was carried by the missionaries into those far regions and is still today the church's emblem. It has a crown on the top, with two rounded projections on either side to represent the two natures of Christ. Three rounded projections on each arm symbolize the Trinity, and a large circle in the center represents the sun (light), a symbol widely used by the ancient Assyrians.

At times the Church of the East has been called "Chaldean" because its center was long in the region south of ancient Assyria and known as Chaldea. In modern usage, however, the name Chaldean refers only to the Catholic Uniates who separated from the much weakened and rapidly declining mother church in 1552, and to the community of a few thousand members in South India who have retained a somewhat tenuous relationship with the Church of the East since the era of its great missionary expansion.[7]

The name "Nestorian," although used by the Church of the East itself for many centuries, is now regarded by them as objectionable. It implies that Nestorius was their spiritual father, whereas they had been a self-conscious Christian community for generations before he was born. Nestorius, moreover, was not an East Syrian prelate as such, but Patriarch of Constantinople from 428 to 431. The Christological viewpoint held by Nestorius, and shared by the Church of the East, was branded heretical at the Council of Ephesus in 431. The issue had to do with the relationship between the two natures (human and divine) in the person of Christ. The "Nestorian" position is dyophysite, i.e., recognizing two natures in Christ (as do Catholics, Protestants, and Eastern Orthodox as well), but to the extent that those natures are regarded as quite separate and distinct. In the "Nestorian" view, Mary is not *Theotokos*, the "Mother of God" (Christ's divine nature), but of his human nature only. This is not to question Christ's divinity—and the Church of the East has never questioned it—but to oppose the orthodox doctrine that the two natures were inseparable in the one person at the time of his birth. It is to say that the entirely human Child of Bethlehem became the God-Man at a later point in his earthly life. Thus the term "Nestorian" was used pejoratively by their fellow Christians in both East and West, and people understanda-

21

bly dislike being called heretics.

The adjective "Assyrian" was added to the official name of the Church of the East in quite recent history. It was encouraged by Anglican missionaries, whose dedicated ministry among these people began in 1842, as an acceptable alternative to the largely pejorative "Nestorian." Confined for the most part at that time to the mountain fastness of northern Iraq, the Church of the East was even then a much reduced remnant of its former greatness. It was struggling against both external and internal forces to further divide it, and its people seeking a measure of political autonomy to retain their identity. The term "Assyrian" as a matter of fact has neither religious nor political significance. There is no Assyria in the modern world. Instead, the word reflects ethnic pride and political wistfulness, a fact that did not escape the attention of Iraqi authorities who were determined in the 1930s to brook no real or imagined threat to their power. And the troubles of this unfortunate people have been compounded ever since.

The late patriarch, Mar Ishai Shimun XXI, was forced to leave Iraq in 1932. After spending six years in Cyprus, he established his residence in the United States where he remained until his death in 1975. A dissident minority of the flock in Iraq elected a rival patriarch in 1968 with the encouragement of the Iraqi government. He died only one year later, but has been succeeded by another. Mar Shimun was not permitted even to visit Iraq again until 1970. During that visit he was granted no permission to reestablish residence there, and he failed to heal the breach in the patriarchal office. The present legitimate patriarch of the church is Mar Denkha, former Bishop of Iran. Mar Denkha remained briefly in Iran after his consecration in 1976. He then attempted unsuccessfully to establish his headquarters in Iraq, its logical location for historic and pastoral reasons. Following the pattern of his immediate predecessor he took up temporary residence in Chicago, but has since returned to Teheran.

Liturgical services of this church are conducted in the Eastern dialect of classical Syriac. (Modern or colloquial Syriac was put into written form only in the nineteenth century by Protestant missionaries.) The Liturgy of the Holy Apostles, dating from sometime prior to A.D. 431, is surely one of the oldest forms of worship used by any church in the world today. Most of the faithful partake of the Eucharist only on important feast days. It is served in two parts: wine by the deacons, bread by the priests. Holy Leaven, a piece of dough kept from each baking, symbolizes the continuity of communion bread since the Last Supper in Jerusalem when John the Apostle is said to have kept a piece of the bread served there.

Both priests and deacons marry, even after ordination, and may remarry if their wives die. Clerical celibacy was abolished by the Synod of Seleucia in 499, and during the sixth century even bishops and patriarchs married. A century later, however, obligatory celibacy for the hierarchy was reintroduced and obtains today.[8] Accession to episcopal office was for several centuries hereditary (uncle to nephew), a system introduced in times of such persecution that it was necessary in order to assure the continuation of a hierarchy. Those destined to that office ate neither meat nor animal products from the time of their childhood, except for eggs, milk, and cheese. Both customs were abolished by a synod that met in 1973.

The Assyrian Church of the East uses neither images nor icons. A stand, holding a copy of the Gospels and covered with a cloth, bears a simple cross that is venerated with the kiss of peace that people in other Eastern churches accord to their icons. The simplicity of their church interiors may reflect a concession to the Islamic objection to religious pictures in places of worship, or it may merely attest to the poverty of an isolated Christian people. The former explanation is suggested by their long and uneasy coexistence with the Muslim majority, the latter by the lack of any pronouncements against icons in their decrees.

This church of probably no more than 150,000 members worldwide has a total of six dioceses: two are in Iraq[9], one in eastern Syria, one in Lebanon, one in Chicago, and one in Modesto, California. The diaspora in the West (U.S., South America, Europe, and Australia) accounts for more than half the total membership. Emigration from Iraq and, since 1981 from Lebanon, is unremitting. Slow erosion continues in both Iraq and Iran from conversions to Islam for prudential reasons, and among the diaspora in the "melting pot" of the West where new generations forsake the church of their parents or are lost to it through intermarriage. Elementary schools are maintained by the church in Iraq, Iran, Syria, and Lebanon. This assures some knowledge of the Syriac language among each new generation of children. But a major problem is the lack of theological education for the priesthood.

Anglican and Protestant missionaries in Iran and Iraq, beginning in the first half of the nineteenth century, tried to revive and strengthen the Church of the East with limited success. The early missionaries seem to have regarded this ancient church as in some sense "crypto-Protestant" because of its antipathy to Roman Catholicism (caused mainly by the enormous loss of its membership to the Chaldean Catholic Uniates), and because no icons were venerated in its worship. Consequent associations with the Protestant churches may explain the fact that the Assyrian Church of the East joined the World Council of Churches in 1943, when that council was still in process of formation and several years before it was joined by any of the Orthodox churches.

A tribute paid years ago to this struggling remnant of a once large and prestigious church has lost none of its poignancy:

> From the very start the Nestorian Christians have always been a minority in the lands of other faiths; throughout history they have been subject to persecution and oppression; there has never been a time, except for a while under the Ilkhans, when it would not have profited them to renounce their faith. Such steadfastness is an example for all time, an eternal testimony to the glory of a faith for the sake of which all else is counted well lost.[10]

III. Oriental (Non-Chalcedonian) Orthodox Churches

Four churches belong to the Oriental or "non-Chalcedonian" Orthodox family: Armenian, Coptic, Ethiopian, and Syrian. Their break with the Eastern Orthodox mainstream occurred at the fourth ecumenical council, meeting at Chalcedon in A.D. 451,[11] just twenty years after the Church of the East had repudiated the Council of Ephesus. Thus began the process of division that has plagued much of Christian history ever since. At Chalcedon the theological issue was once again the relationship between the human and divine natures in the person of Christ. The non-Chalcedonian position is sometimes—and, I believe, erroneously—called "monophysite," i.e., one nature only, the divine absorbing the human. In fact none of the Oriental Orthodox churches denies the incarnational mystery of a Christ who is both human and divine, but they strongly object to the "Nestorianism" of the Church of the East (see description in II, above) and they fear that the Chalcedonian definition leans in that direction.

In the world at large, the combined membership of the Oriental Orthodox churches is much smaller than that of the Eastern Orthodox complex. But in several countries of the Middle East and in Ethiopia, the Oriental Orthodox are by far the majority of the Christian population. The Coptic and Ethiopian churches alone have some

24

thirteen million members. Indeed the Ethiopian church is larger than any branch of the Eastern Orthodox family as well, except for the churches of Russia and Romania.

For many centuries the non-Chalcedonian churches lived more or less in isolation from the rest of Christendom and, for political and linguistic reasons, even from one another. They have drawn somewhat closer together in fellowship and joint planning since 1965 when the late Emperor Haili Selassi I invited the patriarchs of all four churches to meet in Addis Ababa. Systematic continuation of the work begun at that meeting would greatly strengthen their family solidarity.

A. The Armenian Apostolic (or Orthodox) Church

A vast majority of the six million Armenians scattered throughout the world today belong to the Armenian Apostolic Church. Perhaps no other people continue to find the church more central to their ethnic life than do Armenians. Even in this day of rapid secularization everywhere, the church remains the focal center of everything that is culturally, religiously, and politically theirs. So long as there are Armenians, the name of St. Gregory the Illuminator (ca. 240-332 A.D.) who made them the first Christian nation, and of St. Mesrob Mashtotz who invented the Armenian alphabet, leading to an early (A.D. 406) translation of the Bible into that language—these and many others will be hallowed. And the untold hundreds of thousands who have been martyred for their faith throughout the long history of this people will remain the symbol of what it means to be an Armenian.

The origins of the Armenian Church are traced in its traditions to apostolic times. St. Thaddeus and St. Bartholomew are venerated as the earliest "Illuminators of Armenia." Christianity became the state religion of Armenia with the conversion of King Tiridate the Great at the beginning of the fourth century (A.D. 301) under the dynamic leadership of St. Gregory called the Illuminator, hence the name "Gregorian" often used of this church. That was a decade before Constantine's edict of toleration and long before there was any state church as such in the Roman realm.

The first construction of their cathedral at Echmiadzin (near Yerevan, the capital of today's Soviet Republic of Armenia) was completed in A.D. 303. It has been rebuilt many times since, but always in the same location. The See of Echmiadzin declared complete independence from Constantinople in A.D. 365, a heritage that may help to explain its alignment two centuries later with the non-Chalcedonian churches against the imperial forces of Byzantium. Less than a century after becoming a Christian state, Armenia was divided between the Byzantine and Sassanid empires, and has enjoyed only a few brief centuries of national autonomy since then. Dominated by other powers, and often massacred and dispersed (from Constantinople, Erzeroun, Van, Sivas, and Aleppo in 1895; from Adana in 1909; from Smyrna in 1922, and so forth), the tragic history of this courageous people explains their persistent desire to reestablish a national homeland. The Soviet Republic of Armenia, where about one-third of all Armenians live today, cannot in any sense be called a sovereign state. Moreover, its territory covers only part of the area once known as "Greater Armenia." Cilicia or "Lesser Armenia" is today a part of Turkey from which the Armenians have been ruthlessly excluded.

Catholicos Vasken I at Echmiadzin continues to hold primacy in the church at large. Three other administrative centers have emerged in the course of this people's long history: the Jerusalem Patriarchate in 1311, presently led by Patriarch Yeghishe Derian; the Catholicosate[12] of Cilicia in 1441, now headed by Catholicos Karekin II Sarkissian in Antelias, Lebanon; and the Patriarchate of Constantinople (Istanbul) in 1461, now under the leadership of Patriarch Shnorkh Kalustian. All four are governed by church councils with prominent lay membership, in a ratio of seven laity to three clergy, a system as thoroughly democratic as may be found in any other Christian church.

The real or alleged political "captivity" of Echmiadzin in the Soviet Union continues to plague its relationships with Cilicia. A dispute between the two catholicosates began as early as 1899 over their respective jurisdictions.[13] This was exacerbated after World War I and the rise of the communist regime as the U.S.S.R. It reached a crescendo in 1956, when Echmiadzin attempted to interfere by declaring the election of Zareh I as Catholicos of Cilicia nul and void. As a result of this long-standing dispute the Cilician Catholicos, whose jurisdiction was formerly limited to the faithful in Syria, Lebanon, and Cyprus, extended it to the three dioceses in Iran as well as to certain dioceses in Europe and North America. Some reconciliation has taken place beginning with the 1963 meeting in Jerusalem between Vasken I of Echmiadzin and Khoren I of Cilicia. Meanwhile Echmiadzin's "primacy of honor" continues to be acknowledged throughout the church and reiterated in every liturgical celebration. But the Cilician

Catholicosate (now in Antelias, Lebanon) claims equality in administrative authority.

Political differences among the Armenian people are reflected in three parties that have arisen within their church:[14] Henshak, founded in Geneva in 1888, has a Marxist orientation and champions a return of the people to Soviet Armenia; Tashnak, founded also in Geneva two years later, in 1890, has a rigorously anti-communist stance; and Ramgavar, founded in Istanbul in 1908, holds a position close to that of Henshak. It is due to radical elements within these parties that violent attacks have been made in recent years against Turkish diplomats in particular. Such attacks are of considerable embarrassment to both catholicosates, and especially onerous to Patriarch Shnorhk Kalustian in Istanbul who personally deplores them and whose fragile relationships with the Turkish government are jeopardized by them.

The Armenian Apostolic Church today has a total of twenty-eight dioceses under the two catholicosates. The seventeen under Echmiadzin (with considerably more than half the total membership of the church as a whole) are as follows: five in Soviet Armenia and elsewhere in the U.S.S.R. (Ararat, Shirac, Georgia, Azerbaijan, and Nor-Nakichevan); three in Europe (France, England, Austria); two in the U.S.A. (New York and Los Angeles); two in South America (Argentina and Brazil); and one each in Egypt, Iraq, the Far East (Calcutta), Canada, and Australia. The faithful in Palestine and Turkey are governed, as indicated above by the Patriarchates of Jerusalem and Constantinople respectively. The eleven dioceses subject to the Catholicosate of Cilicia are: three in Iran (Teheran, Tabriz, and New Julfa); two in Syria (Damascus and Aleppo); two for the U.S. and Canada (New York and Los Angeles); and one each in Lebanon, Cyprus, Greece, and Kuwait (the Armenians living in the Arabian Gulf Sultanates and Emirates).

The Armenian liturgy was developed early in the Christian era. It drew from the traditions of both Antioch and Byzantium, within a framework of the Jerusalem tradition. Classical Armenian continues to be the liturgical language, but sermons are given in the modern tongue. The hauntingly beautiful music is to some extent of more recent origin, the composer Magar Yegmalian (1856-1905) having played a major role. A steadfast reluctance to use other languages than Armenian for this liturgy reflects the passion of the Armenian people to retain their ethnic identity in whatever parts of the world they live. This is not easy to achieve in the pluralistic, multi-national environment of so widely dispersed a people. It is especially difficult

27

amid the cultural and linguistic forces that affect third- or fourth-generation Armenians in the West—or even in the Arab world. But their tireless effort to pursue it explains the fact that a chief emphasis in all parishes and church-related schools is instruction in the Armenian language.

Throughout the Middle East primary and secondary schools, orphanages, hospitals, sanitaria, and homes for the aged are maintained by the Armenian Apostolic Church. Minor seminaries to educate the clergy are found in various dioceses. Major seminaries are located in Antelias (near Beirut), Jerusalem, and Echmiadzin, the three centers that also take major responsibility for publishing Armenian literature. The Armenians of New Julfa (Isfahan, Iran) introduced the art of printing to Persia early in the seventeenth century, and that diocese has once again become a place of serious Christian scholarship and publication in recent years.

The Jerusalem Patriarchate is much reduced in numerical strength since 1947 because of widespread emigration from that area. It has also been troubled by periodic internal difficulties. Yet the patriarchate continues to play a major role (along with the Greek Orthodox and Roman Catholic churches) in the maintenance of the Church of the Holy Sepulchre and other holy places. Handsome new buildings were recently completed for the seminary. These buildings also house a collection of ancient Armenian manuscripts, second in size only to that in Yerevan and a boon to scholars who come from all over the world to study them.

Monastic life of the traditional kind, once of great importance in the Armenian Apostolic Church, has declined in recent times. Except for Jerusalem, where the Brotherhood of St. James still numbers some twenty-five monks in residence, the monastic vocation is chiefly to teaching and preaching ministries. The Brotherhood of the Catholicosate of Cilicia has among other activities oversight of the theological seminary at Bikfaya, Lebanon. Ancient monasteries like those in northern Iran and the Armenian Soviet Republic no longer house monastic communities as they did in early centuries. But they remain centers of pilgrimage for thousands of the faithful every year. Nuns in this church have become almost an "endangered species." Only three still live in Istanbul, two of them in old-age retirement—and the Constantinople Patriarchate was at one time a major center for women religious, many of whom went from there to serve in distant parts of the church.

The Catholicosates of both Echmiadzin and Cilicia have been members of the World Council of Churches since December 1961.

Karekin II, the Catholicos of Cilicia has served that council with distinction in Central Committee, in the Faith and Order Commission, and in the Commission on Interchurch Aid. In dialogue with the Eastern Orthodox Churches, both catholicosates sent representatives to the inter-Orthodox conference at Rhodes in 1961 as well as to the subsequent Eastern-Oriental Orthodox discussions held under World Council auspices.

In relationships with the Roman Catholic Church, the earliest contacts in modern times were through Armenian observers at the Second Vatican Council (1962-1965). Khoren I of Cilicia met with Pope Paul VI in Rome in 1967. Vasken I of Echmiadzin, accompanied by the Armenian Patriarchs of Jerusalem and Constantinople, conferred with the same pope three years later.[15] In regional associations with Orthodox, Anglican, and Protestant churches of the Middle East, the Cilician catholicosate has been an active and key member of the Middle East Council of Churches since that council's organization in 1974.

B. The Coptic Orthodox Church

The word "Coptic" simply means Egyptian. It is a corruption of *Aiguptos*, the Greek name for pre-Islamic Egyptian peoples, and is still used by the three major Christian communities—Orthodox, Catholic, and Protestant—in that most populous of all Arab states. To be known as a Copt is to be identified in modern Egypt as a Christian rather than a Muslim. The vast majority (about ninety-five percent) of Egyptian Christians now belong to the Coptic Orthodox Church. In their own tradition, claiming the authority of the historian Eusebius (ca. 260-340 A.D.), the origins of Egyptian Christianity are traced to the first-century residence and martyrdom of St. Mark in Alexandria.

Dioscorus I (died A.D. 454) was an early patriarch of the then undivided See of Alexandria and a chief exponent of the so-called monophysite or "one-nature" Christology at the Council of Chalcedon. He was removed from office and banished by that council, but the Copts in turn murdered his "Chalcedonian" successor in Alexandria a few years later. The result of the ensuing rivalry is the continuing residence in Egypt of two Orthodox patriarchs of Alexandria: one a Greek "Chalcedonian" (see description of the Eastern Orthodox Patriarchate of Alexandria, above), the other Coptic and "non-Chalcedonian."

From the fifth to the ninth centuries the Greek patriarchs occupied the city of Alexandria proper, relegating their Coptic counterparts to rule from one of the desert monasteries. But the non-Chalcedonian party continued to grow steadily. Today the Greek patriarch presides over a still declining minority of Egyptian and expatriate Greek Christians, while the Coptic patriarch heads a flourishing majority of the indigenous faithful, by far the largest church of any denomination in the entire Middle East. Each maintains a residence and patriarchal office in both Cairo and Alexandria.

The Egypt of early centuries was very widely Christianized. But the Arab conquest under 'Amr bin al-As in A.D. 640 began the process that ultimately reduced the Copts from majority to minority. By the eighth century Arabic rather than Coptic had become the official language of the country. Persecution under the Mamluk dynasty (A.D. 1250-1570) further reduced the number of Christians to about ten percent of the total population, approximately the proportion they have managed to retain ever since.[16]

The Copts, living as they do at the intellectual center of Islam, have struggled through the centuries to maintain their identity as a Christian people while at the same time making significant contributions to the wider environment. The modern story of Arab nationalism and of Egypt's emergence from colonial domination is crowned with important figures from the Coptic community.

The predominantly Muslim government of the country even today acknowledges the Coptic contribution to Arab renaissance and defends this people against occasional outbursts of opposition from militant elements within the Islamic population. The recent growth of Muslim fundamentalism in Egypt as well as elsewhere in the Middle East has increased the incidence of such outbursts, and the government's protection of Christian interests has taken a strange turn: The present Coptic Patriarch and 117th successor to the throne of St. Mark, Anba Shenooda III, had been quite vocal in protesting against the violation of property and personal rights of Christians by fanatical Muslim groups. In 1981, the late President Anwar Sadat deprived Pope Shenooda of his authority in the church's temporal affairs, putting him under a kind of "house arrest" at a desert monastery in Wadi'l-Natrun, and requiring a council of five Coptic bishops to administer the legal and financial matters of the church.

The church continued to recognize Shenooda as patriarch and spiritual leader, and later appealed through its bishops to a higher court to have his temporal authority restored. The decision of that court in March 1983 upheld the earlier restrictions placed on Shenooda's activities, but overruled the requirement that legal and financial administration be restricted to the authority of the five-bishops council. A widespread and probably accurate interpretation of the issue is that it reflects the Egyptian government's need to maintain a balance in dealing with religious unrest in the country. If they are to contain the activities of Muslim extremists—and it is certainly in their political interests to do so—they must also appear even-handed by curtailing the authority of the most influential and outspoken representative of the largest Christian minority in the population. Pope Shenooda was released and resumed all his patriarchal functions in 1985. Yet the very fact of the government's interference in Coptic Orthodox affairs has a troubling effect on all Christians in Egypt.

The Coptic Orthodox Church has twenty dioceses, archdioceses and metropolitanates throughout Egypt. There are also metropolitanates in northern Sudan (Khartoum and Omdurman) and one in Jerusalem. The Metropolitanate of Jerusalem is primarily a monastic community involved with this church's historic responsibility in the care of certain holy places, but church congregations and schools are in Jerusalem, Bethlehem, and Jericho. The Archbishop of Jerusalem also has oversight of the much larger number of Copts living in Kuwait, Iraq, Jordan, Gaza, the Sinai, Abu Dhabi, Bahrain, Lebanon, and the Emirates of the Arabian Gulf. The upper clergy in all those countries report directly to him.

In recent years, with the large emigration of Egyptians to Libya and the North African Maghrib, the ancient Bishopric of the Five Cities has assumed growing importance. The Bishop of Copts in North Africa ("the Five Cities") resides at Damenhour in the Nile Delta. His responsibilities include the oversight of two congregations in Libya served by priests from Egypt, and smaller communities of Coptic Orthodox people in Algeria and elsewhere who are currently without resident priests.

Monasticism is even yet a more dominant force among the Coptic Orthodox than in any other church of the Middle East. To be sure there are only nine monasteries left,[17] with a total of no more than three hundred resident monks, and five convents with about one hundred nuns. Yet the monastic spirit dominates the theological thought and ecclesiastical leadership of this great church. Bishops and patriarchs are still selected exclusively from the monastic communities, and Coptic Orthodox piety continues to reflect the monastic tradition of the desert.

The church's major seminary is in the Abassiya section of Cairo, adjacent to St. Mark's cathedral and the patriarchal offices. This seminary was established in 1893 and has been on its present site since 1953. About fifty percent of all the parish priests are educated

31

there, and large evening classes enroll lay people interested in biblical and theological studies. Comparable evening sessions for the laity are also held in Alexandria and Tanta. A Coptic Institute of Higher Studies was founded in 1954 at the Cairo patriarchal compound and has become an important ecumenical center for the study of Coptic language, literature, music, art, and liturgy. A Coptic Archaeological Institute is located nearby.

Among current developments of special note in this Coptic church is the growing emphasis on Bible study. Each week, usually on Friday afternoon, scores of parish churches are crowded with people for this purpose. The largest such gathering is the weekly Bible study led by Pope Shenooda at St. Mark's Cathedral in Cairo. An attendance of six thousand, mainly young people, is not uncommon.

A close relationship between the Coptic and Ethiopian Orthodox Churches has existed for many centuries. Until 1951 all bishops for Ethiopia were appointed by the Coptic Patriarchate, and the official title of the Coptic Patriarch was "Pope of Alexandria and Patriarch of the See of St. Mark in Libya, the Five Cities of the West and the Lands of Egypt, Abyssinia and Nubia." It was not until 1958 that the strong nationalistic spirit of independence in Ethiopia succeeded in establishing a fully autocephalous church under its own patriarch. Yet the historic ties were not entirely severed, and each church still enjoys a position of influence in the life of the other. Today the Ethiopian Church, with an estimated membership of eight million, is much larger than any other church in the Oriental Orthodox group. The current political climate in Ethiopia puts that church's future in some jeopardy, however, and limits its associations with the Coptic patriarchate. The revolutionary Ethiopian government forceably removed the Ethiopian patriarch from office and imprisoned him in 1976. The Coptic Synod registered its protest by refusing to send any representatives from Egypt to the consecration of his successor.

Isolated for many centuries from both Latin West and Byzantine East, the Coptic Orthodox Church is presently involved in ecumenical relationships at international, regional, and local levels. It has been a member of the World Council of Churches since 1954, and since 1956 a leader of the Ecumenical Advisory Council for Church Services (EACCS) in Egypt. Since 1962 one of the Coptic bishops has devoted full time to the Office of Public, Ecumenical and Social Services at the patriarchate in Cairo. In 1974 the Coptic Orthodox became a founding member of the Middle East Council of Churches (MECC) and continues to play a leading role in the activities of that regional body. Yet, as is the case with most other churches in the Middle East, the vast membership in village churches is still relatively untouched by any kind of interchurch relationships.

C. The Syrian Orthodox Church

The ancient and venerable Syrian Orthodox Church traces its ancestry to the earliest days of the once undivided Antioch Patriarchate. According to tradition, the Apostle Peter founded this church in Antioch around A.D. 37 and is therefore regarded as its first patriarch. The present incumbent, Mar Ignatius Zakka I Iwas, is said to be the 122nd in the line of succession. After the Council of Chalcedon in 451, this Syrian Church separated from Byzantine Orthodoxy because of the Christological issue raised at that council (see the first paragraph of Section III, above). It is a church of unquestionable apostolic foundations, and an important member of the family of churches now called Oriental Orthodox.[18]

In A.D. 543, nearly a century after the Chalcedon Council, a monk named Jacob Baradeus (Yacoub Bourd'ono) was secretly consecrated a bishop by Theodosius, the Patriarch of Alexandria and a leading figure in the protest against the Chalcedonian formula. Baradeus traveled widely in the anti-Chalcedonian cause and against the imperial establishment—through Syria and Asia Minor, to Armenia, Cyprus, Egypt, even to Persia. He is said to have personally consecrated twenty-seven bishops and thousands of priests and deacons. The Syrian Orthodox credit him with having brought a revival of strength to their church, then already much depleted by a century of imperial persecution. It is because of Jacob Baradeus's great influence in their history that these Syrian Christians have been nicknamed, somewhat derisively, "Jacobites."

The Syrian Orthodox remain close to the Jerusalem tradition of the early church. Classical Syriac is still their liturgical language, and they attribute the composition of their liturgy to St. James, brother of our Lord and "the first Bishop of Jerusalem." The western dialect of the Syriac they use is, they claim, very close to the language spoken by Jesus. It was the mother tongue of the Aramaean majority in pre-Islamic Syria, a country widely Christianized in early centuries. According to the church's current patriarch, Syriac and Aramaic are identical. The former term came to be used by the early Christians of Syria, the latter by the dwindling pagan population in that land.[19] Syriac continues to be the basic medium of communication in some of the Syrian Orthodox villages of Iraq and eastern Turkey. That, however, is a modern Syriac which like all other languages has changed with the times. And the struggle to maintain it amid the growing pressure of Arabic and Turkish educational systems is not easy.

During the fourth and fifth centuries, membership of the Syrian Orthodox Church of Antioch extended from the western provinces of the Byzantine Empire eastward into Persia. But its numerical strength was depleted from the sixth century onward for a variety of reasons: The rapid spread of Islam took its inevitable toll. There were also defections to the "Melkite" (Chalcedonian) Orthodox fold under political pressures. On its eastern flank the church was further divided by Persian support given to the Nestorians against Antioch (see Section II, above). And, beginning in the eighteenth century, considerable numbers were lost to the Syrian Catholic Uniates.

The Syrian Orthodox made enormous contributions to Christian scholarship in early centuries from their centers in Antioch, Nisibis, and Edessa. In 559 the see of a Catholicos subject to the Antioch Patriarchate was established at Tikrit in Mesopotamia, eastward of the Roman realm. There the "Golden Age" of scholarship reached its peak in the thirteenth century through such notable theologians as Gregory Bar Hebraeus (1226-1286). That catholicosate continued until 1860, when it was abolished because the size of the flock under its jurisdiction no longer justified its separate existence. The patriarchate itself, following exclusion from Antioch proper in A.D. 518, was moved from place to place in Syria for several centuries. In the thirteenth century it was located at the monastery called Deir Zafaran near Mardin (now in Turkey). In 1933 it was taken to Homs, Syria, and in 1959 to its present site in Damascus.

The Syrian Church sent early missionaries into Asia Minor, the Syrian desert, Palestine, Armenia and the Caucasus, Persia, the Arabian peninsula, and even to South India and China. This missionary movement was later frustrated by the church's progressive isolation under Muslim rule, and by further reductions in strength as a result of massacres. The Kurdish retaliations of 1843, 1846, and 1860 took a heavy toll. And from 1909 until the 1920s the Syrian Orthodox shared the fate of Armenians and Greeks in the ruthless determination of the Young Turks to eliminate whatever minorities seemed a threat to the political policies of pan-Turanism ("Turkey for the Turks"). The Syrians, like the Armenians, had sought an independent "homeland" free of Turkish rule, and that was the occasion for the massacre of many thousands in the regions of the modern Turkish state after the collapse of the Ottoman Empire.

34

The Syrian Orthodox Church of Antioch now has a total of twenty-six archbishoprics throughout the world. Twelve are in the Middle East: four in Syria (Damascus, Aleppo, Homs, and al-Hasaka); three in Iraq (Baghdad, Mosul, and Basra); two in Lebanon (Beirut and Mt. Lebanon); two in Turkey (Midyat and Mardin); and Deir Mar Markos in Jerusalem (with responsibility for the parish in Amman, Jordan). Among the diaspora in the West, there is an archbishopric for North America (the United States and Canada), two in South America (Brazil and Argentina), and one in Europe (for Scandinavia and the Benelux countries). The remaining ten dioceses are in the Syrian Church of Malabar, South India. This is a large church of more than a million members, but it is unfortunately divided between those loyal to the Antioch Patriarchate and those who recognize only the authority of an Indian catholicos. These two Indian factions have a long heritage in common and regard themselves as a single people, but more than half of them find it difficult to retain the historic ties with the patriarch in Damascus because of the great distance and language difficulties.

In the Middle East, Syrian Orthodox concentrations of population are in process of redistribution. Their constituency in Lebanon greatly increased in the 1950s and 1960s through immigration from other parts of the region. For this reason the diocese of Mt. Lebanon was newly created in April 1973, and new primary and secondary schools were developed under church auspices. Many of the new residents from Iraq and Syria were unable to get Lebanese citizenship, however, and the precarious situation of all non-citizens in Lebanon since 1981 makes their continued residence there uncertain. In Iraq, where this church has been since very early centuries, a continual migration of Christians from Mosul in the north has brought the majority of Syrian Orthodox into the diocese of Baghdad. Yet some villages in the north, one of the largest being Bartolla, maintain a solidly Christian and predominantly Syrian Orthodox population.

A more serious erosion continues to afflict the Tur Abdin area of southeastern Turkey.[20] Numbering forty thousand only one generation ago, Christians in the towns and villages of Tur Abdin are now less than eight thousand, most of them middle-aged or elderly. Centuries ago in this "homeland" of Syrian Orthodox monasticism, the hillsides of Tur Abdin were dotted with monasteries housing several thousand monks. Two large monastic compounds and a few smaller ones remain, but the company of monks is now less than a dozen in total. Five are at Deir Zafaran (eighth century) near Mardin, and four at Deir Mar Gabriel (fourth century) some twenty miles east of

Midyat. The others have been sent one by one to care for a few smaller buildings that have not been allowed to fall into disuse. The latter lead a lonely life, separated not only from their fellow monks but from Christian communities altogether. Nuns only slightly outnumber the monks. Ten of them are at Deir Mar Gabriel, one at Deir Zafaran, two at Deir Mar Yakoub near Salah, and one at Hakh.

Theological education for the Syrian Orthodox clergy is to some extent still provided by the monasteries. Along with Deir Zafaran and Deir Mar Garbiel in Turkey, and Deir Mar Markos in Jerusalem, all mentioned above, mention should also be made of Deir Mar Matta near Mosul, Iraq, where three monks still reside. Dating from the fourth century, it is said to be the oldest monastery of any church in that country. However, the major training center for the priesthood is now the patriarchal clerical school of Mar Ephrem. Founded in 1939 at Mosul, Iraq, the school was moved for a brief period in the 1960s to Zahle in Lebanon's Bekaa Valley. In 1968 new buildings were erected in the Lebanese village of Atchaneh, near Beirut. There it grew in enrollment and strength of academic program until the intensity of the Lebanese civil war forced removal of the students to Damascus.

Today the Syrian Orthodox are scattered more widely than ever before across the face of the earth. Their membership is much reduced from the vast numbers of earlier centuries. Yet they continue to demonstrate the remarkable resilience that has characterized their long history. Their youth movement is alive, and signs of renewal are evident in many aspects of the church's program.

IV. The Eastern-Rite Catholic Churches

Over the past four centuries in particular, and for various reasons, some people have separated from all the ancient churches described above to unite with Rome. Eventually they formed Eastern-rite Catholic churches under their own patriarchs. In some cases the bishops of these emergent churches reestablished communion with their respective mother churches for brief periods. But such reconciliations were spasmodic, and in no case was permanent reunion achieved. Two important factors contributed to the separations: the theological controversies inherited from the fourth and fifth centuries, and the missionary activities of Rome from the thirteenth century onward.

Five different Eastern-rite Catholic churches were thus established as new patriarchates in the Middle East between 1552 and 1824: Chaldean Catholics (derived from the Assyrian or "Nestorian" Church of the East) in 1552; Greek Catholics or Melkites (derived from the Eastern Orthodox Patriarchates of Antioch, Alexandria, and Jerusalem) in 1742; Armenian Catholics (derived from the Syrian Orthodox Church) in 1773; and Coptic Catholics (derived from the Coptic Orthodox Church) in 1824. Those five are called Uniate Churches, i.e., united with Rome. A sixth Eastern-rite Catholic body, the Maronite Church, rejects the designation "Uniate" because it claims to have been in communion with Rome continuously since its own foundation in the early part of the fifth century. There is little doubt of uninterrupted solidarity with Rome from the latter part of the twelfth century onward, although the accounts of earlier centuries are not easy to document. Thus the Maronites are clearly Eastern-rite Catholics, but not Uniates in the same sense as the other five churches whose reunion with Rome came after many centuries of alienation.

All six of these churches (as well as other Uniate bodies not represented in the Middle East) are organically related to Rome through the Sacred Congregation for the Oriental Churches. Each of them retains the liturgy of its Orthodox heritage in the respective traditional languages: Arabic, Syriac, and Armenian. A process of Latinization has taken place in the practices and lifestyle of the clergy, more noticeably in some of the churches than in others, but they remain Eastern in the basic character of their life and worship, each with undiminished loyalty to its heritage as a distinctive people. Thus Armenian Catholics are unmistakably Armenian, Chaldean Catholics are just as clearly Assyro-Chaldeans, and so forth.

In most countries where there are Uniate churches, the Roman Catholic Church of the Latin Rite is also present. This is partly because of a necessary ministry to expatriate Catholics. More significantly it is because Latin-rite religious orders, many of which have been in the area for centuries, continue to render valuable service to the region. Many activities of these religious orders, especially in education, medicine, and welfare, are integrated with the life and program of the Eastern-rite Catholic churches. In most places the vast majority of Latin-rite Catholics are people from Europe and America who are residing in the area either temporarily or permanently. However, this church also has some native membership in most of the countries and a predominantly native constituency in several of them.

The Latin-rite Catholic Church will be considered separately, in the next section of this survey.

A. *The Maronite Catholic Church*

The tragic events in Lebanon since 1975 have made the Maronites familiar, in name at least, to millions of people in the West who had never heard of them before. Those same events, however, make it difficult to view the Maronites from any perspective other than that of their political and military audacity. It is the purpose of this brief section to focus on their identity as a church.

Maronite history began at the end of the fourth and early years of the fifth century. St. Maroun, from whom the name of their church is derived, had an important monastic center midway between Aleppo and Antioch in the Syria of that day. St. Maroun's followers developed within the theological and liturgical traditions of Antioch, but as a more or less independent community. Their claim to unbroken communion with Rome is questioned by many historians, yet the fact remains that the Maronites never regarded themselves as being party to the rupture between East and West, and their history is essentially different from that of the Uniate Catholic Churches (Chaldean, Melkite, Syrian, Armenian, and Coptic) described below.

In the ninth century the Maronites sought refuge from the struggle against other Christian communities as well as Muslims, and settled in the mountains of Lebanon. There they have been able to maintain their identity as a people and a high degree of independence ever since. In turn, Lebanon's independence as a sovereign state in 1943, its unique confessional system, and its strong ties with France, owe more to the Maronites than to any other people.

The present Maronite Patriarch of Antioch and All the East is Nasrallah-Peter Sfeir, elected to the patriarchal office in April 1986. His residence is at Bkerke, some twenty-five miles from Beirut, where it was moved in 1790 from the mountain stronghold of Qannubin. The great majority of the church's membership is Lebanese, about five hundred thousand in 850 parishes belonging to eight dioceses in that country: Beirut, Tripoli, Sidon, Byblos-Batroun, Tyre, Zahle-Baalbek, Serba, and Jounié. They constitute the largest church in Lebanon, accounting for about thirty-seven percent of all the Christians and seventeen percent of the total population. More than one hundred primary-secondary schools, eight hospitals, and nine dispensaries are related to this church in Lebanon alone.

The most important minor seminaries are in Tripoli and Ain

Saade. A larger training school for the clergy is at Ghazir where a number of married priests are in the student body. Advanced theological education is provided by the Pontifical Faculty of Theology at the University of the Holy Spirit, Kaslik (USEK—Université Saint-Esprit, Kaslik), midway between Beirut and Tripoli. That rapidly developing institution enrolls Maronite students in the majority but includes some from other Catholic churches in the country, Melkite, Syrian, Latin-rite, and Armenian. With forty-one professors in 1983, Kaslik claimed to have the first truly indigenous theological faculty in the Middle East. St. Joseph University in Beirut also has a department of theology in which Maronite professors collaborate with the European Jesuits. The Maronite College in Rome, founded in 1890, is now a hostel for students attending the Gregorian and other universities there.

The Maronites, staunch defenders of a "Christian Lebanon," include those who openly advocate partitioning the country if that should be necessary to assure that some part of it remains predominantly Christian. Many of the priests and lay people do not share that opinion, but the call for partition does represent a widespread and persistent fear among Maronites of Muslim political control. Lebanese Muslims, on the other hand, understandably resent the Maronite domination of a country in which neither that church alone nor all Christians combined are any longer a majority of the population. Maronite hegemony is a major issue in this sorely troubled country today, and to a large extent other Christian communities share the resentment felt by the Muslims. Yet the Maronites regard themselves as the indispensable custodians of Christian security.

Smaller Maronite populations are found elsewhere in the Middle East: The two dioceses in Syria, Aleppo and Latakia, have a total of about twenty-five thousand members. Most of those are in villages throughout the coastal area, but there are urban congregations in both cities named and in Damascus. In Egypt, about four thousand belong to the Diocese of Cairo. They are concentrated in Cairo itself and in the suburb of Heliopolis, but small congregations are in other parts of the country. The Diocese of Cyprus now has about three thousand members, their largest parish being in Nicosia the capital city. Scattered small groups of Maronites live in Turkey, Algeria, and northern Sudan. But the diaspora in North and South America, Europe, Australia, and elsewhere may now total more than a million, considerably larger than the entire membership in the Middle East. Lebanese who have emigrated over the years to all parts of the world tend to retain their religious identity in their adopted countries. The majority of such emigrants, until recent years at least, have been Christians rather than Muslims. Thus the Maronites and other churches in Lebanon continue to enjoy the loyalty and often the financial aid of vast numbers outside the homeland.

Monastic life in the Maronite Church is similar to that of the Latin rite at the point of decreasing vocations among the cloistered communities and an increasing variety of secular activities for the others. Male congregations are the Lebanese Antonines, the Mariamite Antonines, the Antonines of St. Isaiah, and the Congregation of Lebanese Missionaries. Those four societies currently have a total of three hundred fathers and brothers along with three hundred novices and students in preparation. Some 180 religious sisters belong to the Nuns of the Old Observance and the Visitation Sisters (both of which orders are cloistered), the Congregation of the Holy Family, the Antonine Sisters, and the Congregation of St. Theresa of the Child Jesus. Except for the now declining cloistered communities, these male and female religious societies assume a large part of the responsibility for the church-related schools, hospitals, and welfare enterprise of their church.

Latinization in the Maronite Church is more evident than in most of the other Eastern-rite churches, due probably to the longer association this community has had with Rome. The liturgy, formerly in Syriac and Arabic, is now entirely in Arabic but its form has undergone numerous changes over the centuries through Latin influence. Celibacy of the parish clergy is also general, although there are married priests serving some congregations. The present trend, however, is clearly a reemphasis of the Antiochene heritage. This trend is manifested in movements of liturgical reform, in a reexamination of the role of married clergy and special provision for their education, and in growing associations with other churches of the Antiochene tradition, both Catholic and Orthodox.

B. The Chaldean Catholic Church

The ancient roots of the Chaldean Church are identical with those of the Assyrian Church of the East (see Section II, above).

Roman Catholic efforts toward uniting these people with Rome began at the time of the Crusades, primarily under the Franciscans and Dominicans. In 1289 the famous Franciscan missionary, John of Montecorvino, took a letter to China from Pope Nicholas IV addressed to Yabalaha III, Mongol-born Catholicos of the Church of the East from 1281 to 1317, who was said to have been "well disposed toward the Catholic Church."[21] But conversions to Latin-rite Catholicism throughout the Middle East were sporadic and short-lived, and it was not until the middle of the sixteenth century that a Uniate Catholic Church emerged anywhere in the region.

The Chaldeans have the distinction of being the first Uniate church to be established under its own patriarch, and it is the only one that ultimately became larger than the ancient church from which it separated. In 1552 a part of the Nestorian community refused to accept the hereditary election of Simon VIII Denha as Patriarch of the Church of the East. They sent a monk, Youhannan Soulaka, to Rome where he was consecrated Chaldean Patriarch of Babylon. The term "Chaldean" is said to have been selected by Rome to convey a religious connotation rather than the transparently political intention of the adjective "Assyrian" later adopted by the Church of the East. "Chaldean" suggests the traditional origin of the Magi who came from the East to celebrate Christ's birth.

The line of Chaldean patriarchs that began with Soulaka was by no means unbroken. For the next three centuries, until about 1830, there was an irregular, back-and-forth movement among bishops and patriarchs between acceptance and rejection of Roman authority. The location of the Chaldean patriarchate was also changed from place to place during those centuries: Diarbakir, Salmas, Urmia. More stability was achieved when it was located at Mosul in 1830. Between 1900 and 1947 the Chaldean Catholic membership enjoyed its most spectacular growth, as the political troubles experienced by the Church of the East further reduced the strength of that ancient community. In the early 1950s, when all Christians had begun their migration from northern Iraq toward the capital city, the Chaldean patriarchate was moved to its present location in Baghdad.

The present Chaldean Patriarch of Babylon is Mar Paulos II Cheikho. There are fifteen dioceses of this church throughout the Middle East: eight in Iraq (where it is by far the largest church in the country), three in Iran, and one each in Syria, Lebanon, Turkey, and Egypt. For the widespread Chaldean diaspora in the West there are patriarchal vicars in Australia [2], Canada, France, and Italy (Rome). Some fifty thousand now live in the U.S., and a patriarchal exarch in Detroit is responsible for their local jurisdiction.

The large Syro-Malabar Church in South India with a million and a half members is also Chaldean Catholic. In 1553, just one year after the establishment of the Babylon Patriarchate, the South Indian Church was put under the jurisdiction of that patriarchate by Pope Julius III, but the relationship was broken a half century later. Since then the Indian hierarchy has governed more or less independently of the Middle East, and for much the same reasons as those that separate the Syrian Orthodox Church of Antioch (see Section III, above) from its sister church in South India: geographical distance and language differences.

In the Middle East the Chaldeans celebrate their liturgy in the eastern dialect of classical Syriac. It is essentially an abbreviated form of the ancient liturgy of the Holy Apostles (Mar Addai and Mar Mari) still used by the Assyrian Church of the East. Some Latinization of both format and phraseology has taken place over the years, however, and any residue of the "Nestorian" Christology that is objectionable to Rome has been eliminated.

The historic Chaldean monastic order called the Antonines of St. Hormizdas currently has some thirty-five monks, all engaged in pastoral work. In 1963 another group of six young Chaldean and Syrian Catholic priests in Mosul, Iraq, came together in a semi-monastic community, the Congregation of Christ the King, for joint leadership in lay education and renewal in their respective churches. There are also about 150 Chaldean Sisters of Mary Immaculate in some eight centers in Lebanon, Syria, Iraq, Iran, and Egypt. These are involved in their church's primary and secondary schools, kindergartens, and orphanages. European personnel of two Western communities, the Little Brothers of Jesus and the Little Sisters of Jesus, served under Chaldean auspices at government-operated leprosaria in Tabriz and Mashed, Iran, prior to the 1979 revolution in that country.

Twelve minor seminaries of the Chaldean Church are in Iraq, Iran, Syria, Lebanon, and Turkey. The Patriarchal Seminary at Dora (Bagdhad) was administered by American Jesuits until they were forced to leave Iraq in the late 1960s. That seminary no longer offers courses at the advanced level. Today the only major theological school of this church in the Middle East is the Pontifical Seminary in Mosul, Iraq, where both Chaldean and Syrian Catholic priests complete their training. That institution was directed by French Dominicans until recent years, but it is now entirely under Iraqi leadership. Some Chaldean candidates for the priesthood go for advanced theological study to the University of the Propaganda Fide in Rome.

The good will of the present Iraqi government toward the Chaldeans is expressed in the president's offer of considerable financial assistance to help the bishop in Lebanon replace the prelacy and cathedral destroyed in the recent Lebanese war.

C. The Greek (Melkite) Catholic Church

The literal meaning of Melkite is "the king's people" (from *malka* or *malik*, the Syriac and Arabic words for **ruler**). From the fifth century onward, the theological definitions of the Council of Chalcedon became the official position in both Rome and Constantinople. Hence the non-Chalcedonian Christians referred in a derogatory way to all Chalcedonians as "melkites,", lackeys of the imperial rulers. After the breach between Eastern and Western churches in 1054, that term came to refer more specifically to the Eastern Orthodox (Byzantine) churches in the Middle East as distinguished from the Oriental or non-Chalcedonian churches in the same region. But in modern times it refers exclusively and nonpejoratively to this one Eastern-rite Catholic Church that separated from the Eastern Orthodox Patriarchates of Antioch, Alexandria, and Jerusalem. It was established in union with Rome under its own patriarch in 1724.

This church, like the three Orthodox patriarchates from which it is derived, is not Greek in the ordinary sense of that word. The people are Arabs and the liturgy is Arabic. Its "Greekness" lies simply in the fact that its ecclesiastical and theological backgrounds are entirely Byzantine. In that respect it is different from those Uniate churches in the Middle East that have non-Chalcedonian ancestry—the Armenian, Chaldean, Coptic, and Syrian Catholics.

There were Melkite Catholics long before they had a patriarch of their own. Some Eastern Orthodox bishops had submitted their allegiance to Rome under the persuasion of Roman Catholic missionaries from the sixteenth century onward. Stronger Jesuit and Capuchin efforts to that end began in 1652. In 1684 an Eastern bishop who had professed Catholic allegiance founded the Salvatorian Basilians (still an important religious order in the Melkite Church) to extend Catholicism around Damascus and Aleppo, Syria. But it was Cyril VI (1724-59), a contender for the Orthodox patriarchal office, who began the uninterrupted succession of Melkite Catholic patriarchs. Driven from Damascus by Orthodox opposition, Cyril took refuge in Lebanon at the Holy Savior Monastery near Sidon. There the Melkite Patriarchate remained until Maximos III Mazlum (1833-55) moved it to Damascus, its present location.[22]

The present patriarch is Maximos V Hakim. His official title, and that of his predecessors for the past two-and-a-half centuries, is "Greek Catholic Patriarch of Antioch and All the East, Alexandria and Jerusalem."[23] He resides alternately at each of three centers:

43

Damascus, Beirut, and Cairo. Just prior to his election to the patriarchal office he served for more than two decades (1946-1967) as the Archbishop of Galilee. Throughout those troubled years of Palestinian dispersion and the periodic enlargement of Israel's borders he emerged as an internationally recognized spokesman for the rights of all Arabs living under Israeli jurisdiction.[24] This background in the experience of their current patriarch helps to strengthen the consistently pro-Arab position of the Melkite Church. It also explains the patriarch's personal resolution not to visit Jerusalem at all under present conditions although, as his title suggests, even residence there would be among his prerogatives.

This Melkite Church is, except for the Maronites, the largest and most prosperous Catholic community in the Middle East. Membership is concentrated in Lebanon, Syria, Israel and the occupied West Bank, and Jordan. A smaller but still substantial number of Melkites are in Egypt, and a few parishes are in Turkey, Iraq, and the Arabic-speaking north of Sudan. Throughout the region this church is structured in seven metropolitanates (three in Syria, two in Lebanon, one in Jordan, and one in Egypt), and a vicariate in northern Sudan. Other dioceses have been established for the large and growing Melkite diaspora overseas. Those living in North and South America alone now number more than two hundred thousand.

The parish priests are generally well educated. St. Ann's Seminary in Jerusalem, established in 1882 and long directed by the White Fathers (a Latin-rite order), has unfortunately been closed since the 1960s because of political conditions in the Middle East. It was, however, one of the best theological schools of any church in the region and it may someday be reopened. Meanwhile the White Fathers there continue publication of the prestigious quarterly journal *Proche-Orient Chrétien* and are involved in various scholarly and ecumenical activities. St. Paul's Seminary at Harissa, Lebanon, is directed by the Melkite Paulist Fathers and has now replaced St. Ann's as the church's major training center for priests. Several minor seminaries are scattered throughout the region and are under diocesan or monastic direction.

Iconography is an art in which this church has long excelled. Melkite icons (both Orthodox and Catholic) of past generations are justifiably famous, and newer forms are still being produced by some of the monastic communities. The Paulist Fathers at Harissa in Lebanon are constructing a large and very impressive church in true Byzantine style. It will ultimately house an important collection of Melkite icons, both ancient and modern.

44

Four male religious orders belong to the Melkite Church: the Basilians of al-Shuwayr, the Basilians of Aleppo, the Salvatorian Basilians (with their historic Monastery of the Holy Savior, *Deir al-Mohullus* on the hills overlooking Sidon, Lebanon), and the Pauline Missionaries (Paulists) based at Harissa, Lebanon, near Beirut. Female orders are the Salvatorian Missionaries of the Annunciation, the Basilian Shuwayrites, the Basilian Aleppines, and the Sisters of Our Lady of Perpetual Help. A total of more than five hundred men and women belong to those several communities. They help to staff some fifty church-related primary and secondary schools, six hospitals and dispensaries, and centers to teach manual arts such as sewing and typing. Latin-rite religious and lay societies also send personnel to assist the Melkites with catechetical instruction, parish work, schools, and social and medical services. These include the Franciscan Sisters of Mary (Rome), the Religious of Nazareth (Rome), the Little Sisters of Nazareth (Belgium), and the International Fraternal Association (Switzerland).

This church has given considerable impetus to ecumenical efforts in the region. During the last four decades [25] some members of the Melkite hierarchy have publicly declared a willingness to lead their church into a formal reunion with the Eastern Orthodox patriarchates of its origin if and when intercommunion becomes fact rather than mere possibility. Melkite bishops and priests are also prominent in several widely ecumenical organizations, notably in Lebanon, Syria, and Egypt. Some of the most progressive initiatives have been taken by Fr. Jean Corbon in Beirut and Fr. Xavier Eid in Cairo. Both are foreign-born (Corbon in France and Eid in Belgium), reared and educated in the Latin-rite churches of their native lands, but for many years dedicated and imaginative priests of the Melkite Church in the Middle East. Their unique identification with the cultures of both East and West provides an important bridge for interchurch relationships in their adopted countries.

Few Christian communities in the Middle East are more diversified than the Melkites in their social and political attitudes. Although the membership is largely middle class, and therefore middle-of-the-road in economic orientation, it includes strong and sometimes controversial voices of protest against exploitation of the poor. A case in point is Msgr. Gregoire Haddad, Archbishop of Beirut until 1975. Haddad was charged with heresy (and finally exonerated by Rome), but the real conflict was instigated and continued because of his zealous if sometimes undiplomatic campaign against economic injustice in Lebanon. He remains active in the leadership of an ecumenical but largely Melkite institute in Beirut, the Research Center for Religious Sociology.

These Eastern-rite Catholics are also identified with Arab nationalism and the Palestinian cause, although usually in a somewhat more cautious way than are their counterparts in the Eastern Orthodox Patriarchate of Antioch. An instance in which caution was thrown to the winds, however, occurred in 1974. Msgr. Hilarian Capucci, then Melkite archbishop in Jerusalem, was arrested and imprisoned by the Israelis for allegedly transporting weapons into the West Bank for the Palestinian resistance. The Melkite Synod of Bishops quickly reaffirmed their solidarity with the Palestinian cause despite widespread criticism, within their church as well as outside it, over the particularly militant way Capucci was accused of expressing it. After several months in prison he was released through diplomatic efforts of the Vatican. Although unable for obvious reasons to retain his post in Jerusalem, Capucci lost neither his rank in the hierarchy nor involvement on behalf of his church in the campaign for Palestinian rights.

D. The Armenian Catholic Church

The sixty thousand Armenian Catholics living in the Middle East are clustered mainly in the urban centers of Beirut, Aleppo, Damascus, Istanbul, Cairo, Baghdad, and Teheran, and in secondary cities of primarily Armenian population such as Anjar (Lebanon), Kesab (Syria), and New Julfa (Isfahan, Iran). Smaller parishes are in Amman, Jordan and Jerusalem. Another forty-two thousand are now in the West, chiefly in North and South America and in France.

Like people in the vastly larger Armenian Apostolic Church and the somewhat smaller Armenian Evangelical (Protestant) Union, these Eastern-rite Catholics trace their ancestry to a great Christian kingdom that once stretched from the Caspian to the Black Sea. Those who now live in Soviet Armenia, Iraq, and Iran are for the most part descendants of Greater Armenia in the Caucasus. Those in Syria, Jordan, Lebanon, and Turkey stem from Lesser Armenia or Cilicia (now a part of Turkey from which they have been almost entirely expelled).

A substantial number of Armenian Christians were converted to the Latin-rite Catholic Church, beginning in the fourteenth century, by Armenian Dominicans called Fratres Unitores. Several hundred such Catholics were among the thousands of Armenians forceably transported from Julfa in the north of Persia to Isfahan in the south by Shah Abbas the Great in 1603. A century later there were said to have been as many as ten thousand in Turkey alone. However, the establishment of a Uniate Armenian patriarchate in 1740 assured retention of their familiar liturgy in the classical Armenian language by a church of their own, organically related to Rome.

The first patriarch of the Armenian Catholic Church was Abraham Ardzivian (1679-1749).[26] Ardzivian had been consecrated Bishop of Aleppo in the Armenian Apostolic Church in 1710, but he was obliged to leave that see after a very brief time in office because of this personal attachment to Catholicism. After some years in exile he went in 1739 to the Kreim Monastery in Lebanon where he consecrated three bishops (assisted by Greek Catholic prelates and with the encouragement of the Maronite hierarchy). In 1740 he was elected their patriarch, taking the name Abraham Pierre I. In 1742 he received the pallium from Rome, thus beginning a line of Armenian Catholic Patriarchs of Cilicia, seventeen in number to date, each of whom has used the name Pierre (Peter) in his title.[27]

Kreim Monastery became the first site of the patriarchate, and it was also the mother house of the Armenian Catholic Antonine monks for more than a century after their organization there. When the Kreim buildings were sold in 1865, the patriarch and monks transferred their residence to Beit Khachbao near Ghazir, Lebanon, for two years until 1867. The political situation in the Ottoman Empire then made it desirable for the patriarch to reside in Constantinople, and Beit Khachbao fell into disuse. The Antonine monks then made Bzoummar Monastery near Jounie, Lebanon, their primary residence, as it still is. The patriarch remained in Constantinople until 1920, throughout much of the period of the Armenian massacres in Turkey, when the patriarchate was moved to Bzoummar, some eighteen miles from Beirut. In 1928 it was transferred to Beirut proper, its present location.

Bzoummar alone is left of the Armenian Catholic monasteries in the Middle East. It houses a library of some thirty thousand volumes along with the archives of the church, and fifteen hundred old Armenian manuscripts of which nearly half have been catalogued. There are also some two hundred Arabic, Persian, and Syriac manuscripts in the collection, dealing with religion, medicine, law, and poetry.

The seminary at Bzoummar was first established in 1771, its present classrooms and housing constructed in 1961. Throughout the two centuries of service to date, this school has provided the basic theological education for some fifty bishops of the church and nearly five hundred Antonine monks. The Gregorian University in Rome continues to be used by Armenian Catholic clergy for higher studies.

Armenian Catholic Sisters of the Immaculate Conception are currently 120 in total, living in twenty-three communities throughout the Middle East and in France, the United States, and Brazil. These sisters help to staff fourteen church-related elementary and secondary schools in Lebanon, Syria, Iraq, and Iran, and several homes for the aged. The church offers no medical services at present, but plans are under way to build a clinic in Lebanon.

The Mekhitarians, an Armenian monastic order of Benedictine discipline, was founded in Europe in 1701—forty years before the Uniate patriarchate as such had been established. The Mekhitarians now have two centers: in Venice (San Lazzaro Island) with forty monks, and in Vienna with twenty-four. These renowned communities, although Catholic in affiliation, serve the entire Armenian people through religious and scientific scholarship and in the preservation of their ethnic culture.

The present Armenian Catholic Patriarch (since 1976) is Jean Pierre XVII Gasparian. This church has seven dioceses in the Middle East: two in Syria and one each in Lebanon, Iraq, Iran, Egypt, and Turkey. Patriarchal vicars are in Jerusalem and Amman, Jordan. There are also three organized dioceses among the diaspora in the West: one for North America (the United States and Canada), one in France, and one in Brazil.

Generally good relationships exist between Catholic and Orthodox Armenians, their strong ethnic ties transcending all other loyalties. Intermarriage is common, sometimes with joint participation of the clergy in the ceremonies. Ecumenical activities include the Armenian Protestants as well, bringing these three ecclesiastical communities into contact with one another to an extent unmatched by any other ethnic group in the Middle East.

E. The Syrian Catholic Church

Roman Catholic influence was intermittently strong in certain segments of the Syrian Orthodox hierarchy from the time of the Crusades. Some Syrian bishops were receptive to Roman initiatives toward union, but resistance was always stronger among the parish priests and their flocks. In 1444 a Syrian Orthodox patriarch led his church briefly into communion with Rome, but it was soon interrupted. Nearly two centuries later, in 1622, the arrival of Jesuits and Capuchins in Aleppo, Syria, a stronghold of Syrian Orthodoxy, strengthened the Catholic missionary effort among these people. By

1782 Michael Jarwa, a Syrian Orthodox Archbishop of Aleppo who had personally professed Catholic faith eight years earlier, became a contender for the patriarchal office in his church. But the opposition of a strongly anti-Catholic rival forced Jarwa to flee to Sharfa in Lebanon. At Sharfa, in 1783, he became the first in a continuing line of Syrian Catholic patriarchs.

The Syrian Catholic Patriarchate was transferred from Sharfa to Aleppo a half-century later, in 1831. But within two more decades, in 1850, an anti-Christian uprising among the Muslims of Aleppo forced its removal to Mardin (now in Turkey), also the seat of the Syrian Orthodox Patriarch at that time. Following the Turkish massacres of 1914-1918, thousands of Syrian Catholics along with their Orthodox counterparts emigrated into Syria, Iraq, and Lebanon. Finally, in the early 1920s, Patriarch Ignatius Ephrem Rahmani moved the Syrian Catholic patriarchal see to its present location in Beirut. A permanent residence was constructed by Cardinal Tappuni in the Furn al-Shabbak section of that city in 1932.[28]

Ignatius Gabriel Tappuni was undoubtedly the most remarkable figure in the recent history of the Syrian Catholic Church. Tappuni was the church's patriarch for nearly four decades from 1929 until his death in 1968. He was named a Cardinal in 1936, and it was primarily through his efforts that this church rose from the desolation of World War II to a level of considerable strength and prosperity.

Tappuni's successor, Mar Ignatius Antoine II Hayek is the present Syrian Catholic Patriarch. With a total membership in the Middle East of about one hundred thousand the church has four dioceses in Syria, two in Iraq, and one in Egypt. Patriarchal vicariates are in Lebanon, Jordan, Turkey, and Sudan, and there is a substantial diaspora in the Americas and elsewhere in the West. The large Syro-Malankara Church in Kerala State, South India is historically related to this particular branch of the Antioch Patriarchate.

Male monasticism is not an important emphasis among Syrian Catholics, but there are some monks at Sharfa in Lebanon (now the summer residence of the patriarch), and a few in northern Iraq where, in the Mosul area, there are still some villages of almost solidly Syrian Catholic population. Several Syrian Catholic priests at Mosul follow a semi-monastic discipline jointly with Chaldean Catholic colleagues in the Congregation of Christ the King. They are seeking to promote lay education and renewal in the two churches.

The Ephremite Sisters, a congregation established in 1960, are involved in teaching at several Syrian Catholic primary and secondary schools throughout the region, and in the care of dependent girls. A welfare society has its headquarters at the patriarchate in Beirut. Long-range plans of this church include the development of an industrial training school in the same city.

The Sharfa Monastery in Lebanon oversees the patriarchal seminary and printing press. For students in Syria and Lebanon, more advanced training for the priesthood is provided by the Maronites' Pontifical University of the Holy Spirit in Kaslik, Lebanon. Iraqi candidates attend the Pontifical Seminary in Mosul, a training center shared by Syrian and Chaldean Catholic Churches.

Syrian Catholics celebrate the ancient liturgy of Antioch, retaining a western dialect of the classical Syriac language, but with increasing use of Arabic in the service. Modern Syriac is still a spoken language, particularly in some predominantly Christian towns and villages of eastern Syria and northern Iraq where the Syrian Catholics have substantial membership. Legislation passed in Iraq during the early 1970s makes it possible for all churches of the Syriac tradition there to reinstitute that language as a medium of instruction in their schools. But to maintain it as a spoken language in that Arabic-speaking nation is increasingly difficult and politically unpopular.

F. The Coptic Catholic Church

The early history of the Coptic Catholic Church is a somewhat confused story. There had been Coptic converts to Catholicism since the seventeenth century efforts of Franciscan missionaries in the Holy Land. Nearly a century later, in 1741, the Coptic Orthodox bishop in Jerusalem, Athanasios by name, declared himself a Catholic and was given charge over the scattered groups of Catholic Copts in Egypt by Pope Benedict XIV. But Athanasios, fearful of returning to his homeland in that capacity, appointed a vicar to represent him there.

Being without buildings of their own in Egypt, the Catholic Copts continued to worship in Franciscan churches. In 1824 a patriarchate was actually established for them, but it was short-lived and the leadership again reverted to ordinary vicars. Five years later, in 1829, they were permitted by the Ottoman authorities to build their own churches. In 1895 a Coptic Catholic Patriarchate of Alexandria was firmly established. It was led by Msgr. Cyril Macaire who served as apostolic administrator until he was consecrated patriarch in 1899. Macaire, however, resigned to become a Greek Orthodox in 1908. The Coptic Catholic Patriarchate was again led by apostolic administrators until 1947, when Msgr. Mark Khuzam was elected to the patriarchal office in which he served effectively until his death in 1958.[29]

Msgr. Stephanos I Sidarous was Coptic Catholic Patriarch of Alexandria, with residence in Cairo, from 1958 until his recent retirement. He was named a Cardinal by Pope Paul in 1965.[30] Prior to his election as patriarch, Sidarous served as a theological professor in Europe and was for some years director of his own church's major seminary in Egypt. Son of a former Egyptian Ambassador to the United States, he belongs to one of Egypt's most distinguished families.

This church of about one hundred thousand members is by far the largest Catholic community in present-day Egypt, and the only one that has retained its numerical strength in recent years. The other Catholic churches in that country, both Eastern- and Latin-rite, have a combined membership of less than twenty-five thousand, their numbers having slowly but steadily declined through emigration since the 1960s. There are now six Coptic Catholic dioceses with a total of some two hundred priests: Alexandria (including Cairo), Minia, Assuit, Thebes (Luxor), Sohaq, and Abadir (in the Nile Delta). More than one hundred primary schools, some of them with secondary school classes, are related to the parishes. The church also maintains a hospital in Assuit and several dispensaries, clinics, and orphanages throughout the country.

For all practical purposes the Coptic Catholic ministry is limited to Egypt. No priests have yet been sent to Europe or the Americas, where the church's small diaspora merely participates in the activities of other Catholic parishes. There is, however, a Coptic Catholic priest assigned to the otherwise Latin-rite parish in Tripoli, Libya. Only a few years ago the very large expatriate community of Egyptians in Libya included as many as twenty-five hundred Catholic Copts, most of them professional people and skilled artisans. Their number is now greatly reduced because of political tensions between Libya and Egypt.

The patriarchal seminary of the Coptic Catholics is St. Leo's in Maadi, a Cairo suburb. Most of the church's candidates for the priesthood receive their theological education there, and a few go on to graduate studies in Rome. St. Leo's also provides a valuable ecumenical service as one of the key members in a region-wide association of theological schools now related to the Middle East Council of Churches. The most important minor seminary is at Tahta, midway between Assuit and Sohaq in upper Egypt. The Franciscan fathers related to this church train the members of their order at the

Oriental Seminary in the Giza section of Cairo.

Unlike Coptic Orthodox monasticism where the totally contemplative life continues to play an important role, the more diversified male and female orders of the Coptic Catholic Church are all involved in educational, medical, and welfare activities. In addition to Coptic Jesuits and Franciscans, the Lazarist Fathers have been an established community within this church for a number of years. A more recently organized group of the Dominican discipline is called the Congregation of the Preaching of St. Mark. A female order, the Egyptian Sisters of the Sacred Heart, has a major share in staffing the church's schools, dispensaries, and orphanages.

The liturgy of the Catholic Copts is an abridged form of the longer one still used by the Coptic Orthodox from whom they are derived. Some phrases of the anaphora are still sung in the ancient Coptic language, but the service as a whole is in Arabic. Indeed Arabic scholarship in the composition and translation of theological books is a major contribution of this church today. Coptic Catholics are, no less than their Orthodox counterparts, proudly and self-consciously part of the Arab renaissance.

V. *The Latin-Rite Catholic Church*

Relationships between Rome and the churches of the East were troubled after the fourth century and ruptured in the eleventh. Beginning with the Crusades, Roman Catholic missions influenced the course of Christianity in the Middle East with varying degrees of intensity. A Latin Patriarchate was first established in Jerusalem in 1099 and remained there until 1187. It was then moved to Acre, and the patriarchs resided there until the fall of that city in 1291. After that for six centuries it existed in name only and under titular bishops in Europe. In 1847 this patriarchate was reestablished in Jerusalem and continues to date.[31] Numerous Roman Catholic missionary orders have worked throughout the area, beginning with the Franciscans in the thirteenth century. One response to this impact, as noted in Section IV above, was the emergence of the Uniate churches. Even earlier than those, however, was the establishment of Latin-rite dioceses, some of which continue into the present.

When one speaks of Latin-rite Catholics today, the term does not mean that their liturgy is necessarily celebrated in Latin. That has not been the general practice since the Second Vatican Council.

Whatever vernacular they use, however, the **form** of their liturgy is the one most familiar to Roman Catholics in the West and as such it is different in many respects from the worship patterns of any Eastern-rite churches.

In most countries of the Middle East the majority of Latin-rite Catholics are people from Europe, America, and elsewhere who are residing in those countries either temporarily or permanently. However, the Latin-rite Church has some native members in most of the countries and a predominantly native constituency in several of them. Its situation is so different from one place to another that there seems no way to describe it except country-by-country. Thus it will be necessary to devote more paragraphs to a Christian community of hardly more than seven hundred thousand in total than I have given to some others many times that size. An alphabetical arrangement is for quick reference. It has no relationship to the relative numerical strength or total impact of Latin-rite Catholicism in those countries.

A. *Algeria*

The seventy-six thousand Roman Catholics now in Algeria are almost all expatriates, mainly French. They are a small fraction of the number who were there before independence in 1963, but they constitute almost ninety-five percent of all Christians in the country today. The four geographic dioceses of the colonial period have been maintained, each with its own bishop: Algiers, Constantine, Oran, and Lagouat. A remarkably large number of priests and religious sisters remained in the country after the exodus of other Europeans. Of the 250 French priests, thirty-seven—including Léon-Etienne Cardinal Duval, Archbishop of Algiers—became Algerian citizens. Most of the one thousand sisters (thirty of whom have also taken Algerian citizenship) now serve in government schools, hospitals, and dispensaries.

B. *The Arabian Gulf States*

In the sheikhdoms and emirates that extend the length of the Persian (or Arabian) Gulf, Christians are almost entirely expatriates, and hence their number in a given country is proportionate to the size of the foreign population as a whole. The largest Christian community by far is Indian, and the majority of those Indians are Roman Catholics of the Latin rite.

Kuwait has nearly half the total number of Latin-rite Catholics

53

in all the Gulf States. Its thirty thousand are served by an apostolic vicar and several resident priests.[32] A small group of nuns teach in government schools. A few congregations of Greek Catholics (Melkites) and Maronites have their own priests, but all use the Roman Catholic church building.

In **Bahrain** the Catholic population is concentrated in Manama, the capital city, where they have a rather prominent church building. The resident priests are Latin-rite Capuchins (Franciscans). A dozen or more Verona Sisters serve mainly as teachers in the church-related Sacred Heart School. In addition to the Catholics of Latin-rite background there are many Indian Chaldeans (Syro-Malabar Church), and some Melkites, Maronites, and Syrian Catholics from various Arab countries. Having no resident priests of the Oriental-rite churches, they all attend the Latin-rite services. These are held in English, the only language understood by the Catholic community as a whole.

In **Qatar**, Catholic congregations meet in Doha and at three other centers. An Italian Capuchin is the only resident clergyman of any church in the country. There is no church building, and Christian services are held in the recreation hall of a large oil company's Indian employees. Most of the participants are Indians, but there are some British and a few Arab Catholics from other parts of the Middle East—Maronites, Melkites, Syrian Catholics, Chaldeans—and even a few Orthodox who have no congregation of their own.

Of the estimated five thousand Catholics in **Abu Dhabi** the majority are from India, but there are many Europeans and some Americans as well. About half live in the capital city, and the others are mainly on Das Island, in al-Ain, and elsewhere. An impressive Catholic compound, including a large church building, two church-related schools, and a club house was prominently located on the wide avenue of the Corniche in Abu Dhabi City until 1984. In that year it was torn down and the government provided land elsewhere in the city on which all churches were expected to relocate. The two Catholic schools continue, and they are the only educational institutions under church auspices in the country. One of them, staffed by the Holy Rosary Sisters from Palestine, is taught in Arabic and English. The other, attended mainly by Indian and Pakistani children, is supervised by a small community of nuns from India and is taught in Hindi, Urdu, and Arabic.

In **Dubai** nearly two-thirds (about two thousand) of all the Christians are Catholics. Here also the majority are Indians, but there are Europeans, a few Americans, and some Arabs from other parts of the Middle East. The only resident priest is Latin-rite, and one church building serves all the Catholic communities.

Along with Dubai and Abu Dabhi, five other member states comprise the United Arab Emirates: Sharjah, Ras al-Kaimah, Ajman, Fujeirah, and al-Quwein. Those five were not visited by this writer but are listed here because they are an integral part of the Gulf area. Their combined population is less than five hundred thousand. They are all very traditional Islamic societies, each governed by an autocrat, and with less Western influence than either Abu Dhabi or Dubai. The foreign population includes some Christians in all of them, Roman Catholic in the majority.

Oman has an estimated population of hardly more than nine hundred thousand. Of those only about thirty thousand are expatriates. Hence the percentage of Christians is less then in most of the other major Gulf States. Roman Catholic influence in Oman dates to the Portuguese invasions of the sixteenth century, but the current Catholic constituency of less than one thousand has no resident priest. For several years a visiting priest has come from one of the neighboring countries every two weeks to spend three or four busy days, using the Protestant church building in Muscat or recreation halls in the other centers. This small Catholic community has long wanted to build a school, especially for the Indian children, but has had neither the money nor the government's authorization to begin. In 1973 the ruler of the country gave a piece of land on the outskirts of Matrah, specifying that Catholic and Protestant churches be built there side-by-side. An interchurch committee decided to proceed with the building program and to provide joint upkeep of the property. This is the first Catholic church building to be erected anywhere in the Sultanate of Oman in recent centuries.

C. Cyprus

Cyprus was an important link in Latin-rite expansion during the Crusades. For nearly four centuries (1191-1571) the country was dominated by Catholic powers, especially the Venetians. Most of the one thousand Roman Catholics now on the island are expatriates, but that number includes a vestige of the once substantial native membership.

There are four active parish churches, three in the Greek-Cypriot sector (Nicosia, Limassol, and Larnaca) and one in the Turkish-controlled town of Kyrenia. The latter consists of only a few families and is served on a once-a-month basis by a visiting priest from Nicosia. The churches and schools formerly in Famagusta and Xeros have been closed since the Turkish invasion of 1974.

Cyprus (along with Jordan, the occupied West Bank, and Israel) is an integral part of the Latin Patriarchate of Jerusalem. The patriarchal vicar along with other priests and religious brothers are all Franciscans belonging to the Province of the Custody of the Holy Land, with headquarters in Jerusalem.

The religious sisters who serve the Latin-rite Church of Cyprus belong to three communities: Franciscan Missionary Sisters of the Sacred Heart, Franciscans of the Province of Cyprus, and St. Joseph Sisters. These help to staff four primary-secondary schools in Nicosia, Limassol, and Larnaca with a large enrollment of mainly Greek Orthodox children. The Franciscan Missionary Sisters also maintain a rest home for elderly men and women at Larnaca, and some of them currently teach at a school of the Maronite community at Kornakiti in the Turkish zone.

D. Egypt

The Latin-rite constituency of about six thousand in Egypt is very largely an expatriate community, but some native Egyptian members belong to the parishes. Two bishops (in Alexandria and in Heliopolis near Cairo) coordinate the parish work as well as educational and medical work conducted by some twenty different male and female religious orders. Roman Catholic schools, hospitals, and orphanages have rendered distinguished service to Egypt, some of them for more than a century.

About thirty-five Jesuits of all nationalities including Egyptian fathers are currently involved in a variety of ministries, some of them in collaboration with the Eastern-rite Catholic churches. In Cairo their secondary school, Collège de la Sainte Famille, is large and prestigious.

Nearly a quarter of a century ago Egyptian Jesuit Fr. Ayrout became internationally famous for developing a system of tuition-free primary education in the villages. At its peak this program involved one hundred schools with thirty thousand pupils. During the administration of Egyptian president Gamal Abdel Nasser, the number of these and other private schools throughout the country was greatly reduced. However, the Ayrout Foundation directed by an Egyptian Catholic layman revived an interest in the program, rebuilding it to at least one-third the peak enrollment of the schools and adding dispensaries and community services. An ambitious financial campaign, all within Egypt, has kept Ayrout schools operating and tuition free.

Secondary schools for boys are run by the Christian Brothers, the Lazarist Fathers and the Dom Bosco Fathers. Several Latin-rite orders of sisters are involved with the primary and secondary education of girls, and with hospitals, clinics, and orphanages.

The Franciscan Fathers maintain a Center for Coptic Studies in Old Cairo. Their work is largely independent research, for which they have an excellent library, and they keep in regular touch with the Coptic Orthodox scholars who share their interests.

The Dominican Center for Oriental Studies in Cairo has region-wide importance. Since its establishment in 1934 the major emphasis has been on Christian dialogue with Muslims, and it is one of a very few places in the entire Middle East where such dialogue is pursued systematically. A group of Muslim and Christian scholars meets there every three weeks for joint discussion, currently under the leadership of Egyptian-born Dominican Father George Anawati. Relationships with the Islamic al-Azhar University are cordial and frequent, and both Protestant and Orthodox leaders collaborate. This center publishes the journal *Medio* with scholarly articles useful to Christian-Muslim understanding. The windows in their small but beautiful chapel illustrate only such biblical scenes as are also described in the *Quran*, so that Muslim visitors feel immediately at ease.

E. Iran

The Archdiocese of Isfahan of the Latins governs all Roman Catholic activities in Iran, and it has missionary antecedents that are centuries older then the present archdiocese. Franciscan and Dominican priests first came to Persia in the latter part of the thirteenth century. The Archdiocese of Sultaniyeh which they created lasted no more than a hundred years because of a plague epidemic followed by Tamerlane's invasion. A new missionary effort began in the seventeenth century and the present archdiocese was established in 1632, but again it was destroyed a century later by the Afghan invaders. From 1840 until 1937 Lazarist priests were virtually the only Latin-rite missionaries in the country now called Iran. Several other Catholic orders reentered the country after the second world war.

Until disrupted and reduced in numbers by the revolution of 1979, there were seven thousand Roman Catholics in Iran, largely expatriates. They had four organized parishes, three in Teheran and one in Abadan. Mission congregations were in Isfahan, Shiraz, Mashed, Tabriz, and Rezaiyeh. The Irish Dominicans who headed the archdiocese were obliged to leave the country following the recent establishment of the Islamic Republic. Four different religious orders and societies were involved in schools, medical, and social service institutions. These included a kindergarten, a school for the deaf, fifteen elementary and secondary schools, three orphanages, and three medical dispensaries.

F. Iraq

The Latin-rite community of about twenty-nine hundred in Iraq is composed largely of foreigners but includes a few Iraqi citizens. A Carmelite bishop is Apostolic Administrator.

The Carmelites, called "The Custodians of Iraq," devote much time to the contemplative life and retreats for various age groups. But they also maintain a Christian student center for youth of all confessions and a large primary-intermediate school in Baghdad. Dominicans are involved with scholarly research in both Baghdad and Mosul. In the latter city they were until recently responsible for administering the Pontifical Seminary, the most advanced theological training school for both Chaldean and Syrian Catholic seminarians in the Middle East.

Redemptorist priests serve the few Latin-rite parishes in the country. Dominican Sisters of the Immaculate Conception and Presentation Sisters, most of them Iraqis, help to staff the Chaldean, Syrian Catholic, and Latin-rite schools throughout the country. Until their exclusion from Iraq in the late 1960s, American Jesuits directed al-Hikma University and a secondary school in Baghdad. The Jesuits also taught at the Chaldean Patriarchal Seminary in Dora near the capital city.

G. Israel, the Occupied West Bank, and Gaza

A total of about twenty-four thousand Roman Catholics now live in Israel and the occupied West Bank. Another three hundred or more are in the Gaza Strip. This is one of the few segments of the Middle East in which the Latin-rite Catholic population is largely native and Arabic speaking. More than half of the parish clergy are Palestinians.

In this heartland of the Latin Patriarchate of Jerusalem, Catholic influence is much greater than its numerical constituency suggests. Israel and the West Bank alone have thirty-nine parish churches and worship centers. There are twenty-one male religious orders with a total of 433 members, forty-six female orders with a combined membership of 1,229 and six female lay societies.[33]

Four different theological schools train major and minor seminarians for the secular priesthood and for the various religious orders.[34] Elementary, preparatory, and secondary education is provided by a total of sixty church-related schools.[35] Personnel of the female religious orders also operate children's homes, hospitals, dispensaries, and homes for the elderly. And they help to staff government and private hospitals unrelated to the church.

The Franciscans, known as "Custodians of the Holy Land," continue their historic responsibilities for the Latin-rite care of the holy places, and they have an important Biblical Institute in Jerusalem. The Dominican Ecole Biblique has a very distinguished history in that city.

The Ecumenical Institute for Advanced Theological Studies is at Tantur, midway between Jerusalem and Bethlehem on a campus given for that purpose by Pope Paul VI. Although that Institute is entirely interconfessional in character and administration, Dominicans and Benedictines have had an important share in its development since it was opened in 1971.

Bethlehem University began courses in October 1973 on the site of the Christian Brothers' School in Bethlehem and under the direction of three American priests. This university has a growing student body of about nine hundred, with faculties of liberal arts, sciences, nursing, business administration, hotel management, and teacher training.

H. Jordan

The Hashemite Kingdom of Jordan (east of the Jordan River) is, along with Cyprus, an integral part of the Latin Patriarchate of Jerusalem. The number of Roman Catholics in that country grew after 1948 when many thousands of Palestinians were obliged to emigrate from the territories under Israeli rule. Today their total constituency of about thirty thousand is considerably larger than the number of those who remained in Israel and the occupied territories.

They now have thirty church buildings and worship centers in Jordan, five of them in the capital city of Amman alone. Almost every parish has its own elementary school. The bishop, his auxiliary, and more than ninety percent of the parish priests are Palestinians. In addition to youth activities in the parishes, the diocese maintains campus centers for Catholic students at Jordan University and other state schools.

The personnel of Latin-rite male and female religious orders, although by no means as many as serve in the West Bank and Israel, play an important role in the Catholic educational, medical, and welfare work in Jordan. Four secondary schools, all in Amman, are maintained by the Franciscan Fathers, and Brothers of the Christian Schools. Jesuits are involved in welfare work among Palestinian refugees. Nine female religious orders provide a wide variety of services in the church-related schools, hospital, orphanages, and home for the destitute aged: Sisters of Nazareth, Rosary Sisters, Franciscans of Mary, Franciscans of the Divine Maternity, Sisters of St. Dorothea, Sisters of Nigrizia, Salvatorian Sisters, Sisters of St. Vincent de Paul, and the Missionary Sisters of Charity (Mother Theresa's order).

Arabic is the basic language of the Catholic liturgy in Jordan, but masses are conducted in English for expatriates in the major centers. Two such English masses every Sunday are now necessary at St. Joseph's parish in Amman because of the recent influx of Filipino and Sri Lankan domestic workers.

I. Lebanon

More than half the three thousand Catholics of the Latin rite in Lebanon are expatriates. This community as a whole is vastly outnumbered by the Eastern-rite Catholic churches, especially the Maronites, but it has been fully organized under a Latin-rite bishop in Beirut since 1953. The present bishop is a Lebanese national. He is a member of the Conference of Latin Bishops of the Arab Regions (CELRA) with headquarters in East Jerusalem.

Many of the seventy different male and female Catholic religious orders in Lebanon are of Western origin. About twelve percent of the four thousand fathers, sisters, and brothers are Europeans, and they continue to provide significant leadership for a great enterprise of schools, hospitals, dispensaries, orphanages, homes for the aged, and welfare organizations.[36]

Schools belonging to Catholic churches of all rites educate about twenty percent of the entire school population of the country.

The Regional Secretariat for Near and Middle East of OIEC (The International Office of Catholic Education, with headquarters in Belgium) is located in Beirut. The largest and most prestigious educational institutions are under the direction of Jesuits, Salesians, Marist Brothers, and Brothers of the Christian Schools. Two Jesuit institutions are of particular note: Notre Dame de Jamhour, a boys' secondary school some fifteen miles from Beirut, and St. Joseph University in Beirut. The latter has been one of the most important centers of higher education in the Middle East since it was organized in the 1870s.

The Pontifical Mission for Palestine provides a ministry of welfare, along with industrial and agricultural training, for Palestinian refugees throughout the region. It was founded in Beirut in 1949, and has other local centers in Amman, Jordan and Jerusalem. The Pontifical Mission is largely supported by Catholics in the United States and is presided over by an American prelate. Caritas South Lebanon, a member of Caritas International in Rome, began its relief service to the war-torn southern part of Lebanon in 1972.

J. Libya

Some fifteen hundred practicing Roman Catholics in Libya are the vestige of a community many times that large only two decades ago. They are concentrated in Tripoli and Benghazi, but a number live in the widely scattered oil camps.

In 1970, following the massive exclusion of Italians and other foreigners from the country, thirty-five Catholic church buildings in Libya were confiscated by the government. Three of the four churches in Tripoli itself, including the cathedral, were closed in that way. The one remaining parish church in that capital city now has a constituency of about five hundred. Mass is celebrated there in English, French, Italian, and Arabic. In Benghazi a single Catholic congregation is left. The priests conduct services, teach in a school attached to the Italian embassy, and make pastoral visits to various oil camps in the area.

Nuns of three different religious orders continue to reside in Libya: the Sisters of Mercy (Maltese), the Franciscan Sisters, and the Franciscan Sisters of Mercy (Italian). They now serve in schools and hospitals of the government, all the formerly church-related institutions having been closed after the overthrow of King Idris in 1969.

K. Morocco

Between one hundred thousand and one hundred twenty thousand Catholics, almost all expatriates, belong to the two archdioceses in Morocco, Rabat and Tangier.

Several church buildings have been voluntarily closed in recent years because of the declining European population. However, only the cathedral in Casablanca seems to have been appropriated by the government (for use as a national museum), and that presumably because the church never had clear title to the land on which it was built. Some sixty-two parish churches and worship centers are still used in and around Rabat, Casablanca, Kenitra, Marrakesh, Fez, Meknes, Oujda, and Agadir. Mass is celebrated in French, except for one parish in Rabat and another in Casablanca attended largely by American families. The Tangier Archdiocese is smaller and almost entirely Spanish.

About 175 priests serve the two dioceses, including those who belong to some ten religious orders. A much larger number of sisters in twenty-one religious orders help to staff kindergartens, schools, hospitals, and dispensaries of both church and government.

Primary, secondary, and specialized schools throughout the country are related to the church, but the only religious instruction permitted is Islamic for Muslim pupils. A major seminary in Rabat was closed in the 1960s and the buildings are now used by the government's department of education.

For political reasons, the Berber regions of the country are closed to Catholic institutions of all kinds. A Benedictine monastery formerly in the Berber mountain area refused to move to the coastal area on government demand and relocated instead in France.

L. Sudan

The Roman Catholic population of the northern (Arabic speaking) regions of Sudan is about twenty thousand. These belong to the Khartoum Diocese (established 1913) and El Obeid Vicariate (established 1969) which are almost entirely dependent upon missionary leadership. Few of the ordained priests are native Sudanese. The Comboni (Verona) Fathers and Sisters in this northern area supervise a minor seminary, twelve primary-secondary schools, a technical high school, and a press that serves non-Catholic as well as Catholic churches. A small general purpose hospital in Khartoum is staffed by some of the sisters.

The vast southern provinces of this largest country on the

African continent have an estimated four hundred thousand Latin-rite Catholics, more by far than the combined total of this church's membership in the Middle East and North Africa. The apostolic vicariates of Wau and Rumbek and the apostolic prefectures of Malakal and Mopoi were all established between 1927 and 1955, and the former Juba Prefecture became an archdiocese in 1972. From 1963 to 1971 the political and military turmoil in Sudan deprived these large southern regions of all the former missionary leadership, Comboni and Mill Hill, and of several Sudanese priests.[37] Some sixty organized parishes with a large number of outposts were served by lay catechists, with only two Sudanese bishops and no more than eight ordained priests. A political accord in 1971 enabled some missionary priests, brothers, and sisters to return to the south, and normal pre-war activities were slowly resumed. However, by 1982 new disturbances again jeopardized the activities of all churches in southern Sudan, and the future is uncertain.

M. Syria

Latin-rite Catholics in Syria are, in the majority, native Syrians. Their total number of about ten thousand has slightly declined in the past ten years through emigration. More than half the membership live in and around Aleppo, a concentration dating to the importance of that city as a Crusader center in the thirteenth century. Most of the others are also found in the western part of the country, with strong congregations in Damascus and Latakia.

Male religious orders of the Latin-rite in Syria are Franciscans (the current Apostolic Vicar is a Franciscan), Jesuits, Lazarists, Capuchin Brothers, Marist Brothers, and the Salesians of Dom Bosco. All Catholic schools in which those orders were formerly involved were either nationalized or closed after 1967, when religious instruction and school administration were at issue with the government. Hence the Franciscan priests now in the country (Spanish, Italian, and Syrian) devote all their time to parish work and other activities. Large parishes with a number of expatriates in their membership, such as those in Damascus and Aleppo, conduct masses in French and English as well as Arabic. Jesuit priests in Damascus, Homs, and Aleppo also serve parishes in addition to their work with student groups and a small dispensary. The female orders of Western origin include Franciscans, Missionaries of Mary, Daughters of Charity, Salesians, Congregation of St. Joseph, Carmelites, and Little Sisters of Jesus.

A welfare organization, al-Kalimat Social Work, founded in

Aleppo is now affiliated with Caritas International. This organization operates a hospital recognized as one of the best in the country and a large home for the aged. Five other hospitals and four orphanages are staffed by Latin-rite personnel, some of them in collaboration with the Melkites.

N. Tunisia

Most of the five thousand Roman Catholics in Tunisia are foreigners. The few of Tunisian origin and citizenship participate in otherwise expatriate congregations.

In Tunis, the capital city, there are two church buildings: the cathedral and the parish church of St. Jeanne d'Arc. The cathedral is large enough to have become something of a liability after the decline of the French population in the 1960s. The hierarchy preferred to close it and concentrate on smaller parish churches. They were discouraged from doing so, however, by the government—presumably to dramatize the claim of religious freedom in the country. Six church buildings and three convent chapels are in other towns of the Tunis area: La Goulette, Le Kram, Hamma-Lif, Ez-Zahra, Rades, and Negrine-Coteau. Another eleven churches and twelve small groups meeting in convent chapels or private homes are in cities and towns more distant from the capital: Mateur, Bizert, Tabarka, Kasserine, Grombalis, Nabeul, Sous, Sfax, Gafsa, Metloui, and Redeyef.

About seventy priests and more than three hundred sisters representing a dozen or more religious orders continue to serve in Tunisia. This is a heritage of the colonial era when the church was much larger. Parish work as such now requires only a small number of them, but they are needed to staff some thirty-six institutions still run by the church—schools, agricultural projects, health centers, rural centers, and so forth.

O. Turkey

The presence of Latin-rite Catholics in Turkey, especially those of Italian origin, dates to the Crusades and subsequent commercial involvements. This Catholic community is now much reduced in size, a total of about five thousand of whom less than two hundred are native Turks.

In Istanbul the present bishop is a French Franciscan. His episcopal see is the Eglise St. Louis, a venerable church building in the heart of the city. St. Louis is no longer a parish church, but various activities are conducted there including classes for seminarians of the various Eastern-rite Catholic churches. The four Latin-rite parish churches in Istanbul are St. Esprit (a former cathedral) and three Franciscan churches of St. Antoine, Notre Dame de l'Assomption, and Santa Maria.

In recent years young women of the Focolari movement have helped to lead the parish youth programs in Istanbul. Focolari, organized by Chiara Lubich in the Italian village of Loppiano near Florence during World War II, seems particularly suited to places like Turkey where missionary vocation of the traditional kind is severely restricted. Dedicated young people support themselves in secular employment, but follow a semi-monastic lifestyle. They seek ways to be useful through a low-key and unstructured Christian presence in non-Christian lands.

The Latin-rite Archbishop and Apostolic Vicar of Asia Minor resides at Izmir in southwestern Turkey. His cathedral, the Basilica of St. John, has no continuing congregation but is used by chaplains of the NATO military forces who hold both Catholic and Protestant services there every week. Three parish churches are in Izmir: St. Polycarp with a small French-speaking congregation, Santa Maria, and Notre Dame de St. Rosaire. Other Latin-rite congregations are at Adana, Ankara, Antakya (old Antioch of Syria), Diarbakir, Konya, Mersia, Samsun, and Trabazon. Most of them are served by Franciscan priests. Except for a few primary schools there are no Catholic educational or medical institutions in Turkey.

VI. The Anglican Church

Anglican involvement in the Middle East can be traced to Henry Martyn, a brilliant Cambridge don and linguist, whose entire missionary career lasted only six years, from his appointment as a chaplain of the East India Company in 1806 until his death at age thirty-one in 1812. Martyn's amazing accomplishment of translating the New Testament into the three most important languages of the Muslim world is one of the most remarkable stories in 19th century missionary annals. But the continuing Anglican work must be credited to pioneers of the Church Missionary Society (CMS). Some of these went to Malta in 1815 to print Bibles for use in Turkey and the Arab

Levant. There were also CMS missionaries in Egypt from the early 1820s until they were obliged to leave in 1840. And the work of the Church Missionary Society continues today throughout the region.

Joseph Wolff of the London Society for Promoting Christianity among the Jews (founded 1809) traveled widely in the Middle East from 1821 to 1823. Wolff, the son of a rabbi and a convert to Christianity, was the pioneer in an Anglican mission among Jews.

In 1841 an Anglican bishopric was first established in Jerusalem. Since then, through the efforts of the CMS and the Church Mission to the Jews (CMJ)—now called the Church Ministry among the Jews—small Anglican churches composed of former Muslims and Jews have emerged in various countries of the region. The Jerusalem and East Mission was formed in the 1890s to provide support to the English Bishop in Jerusalem, representing a "middle church" position in contrast to the more evangelical or "low church" character of CMS and CMJ.

The first Anglican Arab bishop was consecrated in 1956 to head the Diocese of Jordan, Syria, and Lebanon. The following year the Anglican see of Jerusalem was made an archbishopric, the English incumbent being carefully designated Archbishop **in** (not **of**) Jerusalem. That title itself underscores the respect Anglicans have long shown toward the Orthodox churches, and an unwillingness even in name to usurp the authority of the Eastern bishops and patriarchs.

For nearly two decades, from 1957 to 1974, the Jerusalem Archdiocese was composed of five dioceses: Jerusalem (including Iraq and Cyprus); Iran; Egypt (including Libya and North Africa); Sudan (including Ethiopia); and Lebanon (including Jordan and Syria). But with the retirement of Archbishop George Appleton in 1974, the archbishopric as such was dissolved, and in its place the Province of the Episcopal Church in Jerusalem and the Middle East was created. The Province has four constituent dioceses: Jerusalem (including Israel, the occupied West Bank, Jordan, and Lebanon); Iran; Egypt (with North Africa, Ethiopia and Somalia); and Cyprus and the Gulf.

A. *The Diocese of Jerusalem*

A total of about thirty-eight hundred members, mostly Palestinians, are in **Israel**, **East Jerusalem**, and the **West Bank**. Congregations meet in Acre, Haifa, Jaffa, Ksfr Jassif, Jerusalem, and Nazareth. Elementary schools are in Haifa and Nazareth, and an important secondary school in Jerusalem. Christ Church, near Jaffa Gate and within the walls of old Jerusalem, claims to be the oldest Anglican church in the Middle East. Christ Church maintains a hostel and an extensive youth program. It has a long-time association with the Church's Ministry among Jews, and a number of "Messianic Jews" (Jewish believers in Jesus as the Messiah) participate in its activities.

In **Jordan** the Anglican total is now some two thousand Palestinians (one thousand others having emigrated elsewhere during the past fifteen years). About half that total belong to the Amman parish alone, the largest congregation in the Diocese of Jerusalem. Three large and prestigious secondary schools in Amman, products of the CMS, are now fully staffed by Arab teachers. The rest of the Palestinian membership is concentrated in smaller Jordanian cities such as Zerqa, Irbid, and Salt. In recent years a Lutheran fraternal worker from Germany[38] was seconded to the Episcopal Church in Jordan.

An Anglican community of twelve hundred (eight hundred Palestinians and Lebanese, four hundred European and American expatriates) was in **Lebanon** just prior to the outbreak of extensive warfare in 1975. The one remaining congregation meets in the chapel of Beirut's Near East School of Theology, an institution the Anglican Diocese of Jerusalem has long supported jointly with several Protestant churches for the theological training of their clergy.

B. The Diocese of Iran

The first Episcopal parish in Iran was established among Armenians at New Julfa Isfahan in 1832. Except for that one small congregation, membership in the Anglican Church in that country has come very largely from non-Christian backgrounds. The diocese itself was constituted in 1912, born of the work of CMS missionaries. Until the Islamic revolution in 1979 it had six organized congregations in Teheran, Isfahan, Shiraz, Yazd, Ahwas, and Kerman. The first Iranian bishop was consecrated in 1961. The Diocese of Iran in collaboration with CMS missionary personnel maintained two elementary and two secondary schools, two hospitals, two youth hostels, a school and farm for the blind, and two bookshops. In June 1979 the diocesan office was moved from Isfahan to Teheran, but efforts to maintain the church's property and structure were in vain.[39]

In accordance with an early agreement, the Episcopal diocese concentrated its activities in the southern part of Iran, while the Evangelical (Presbyterian) Church of Iran worked primarily in the north. Those two bodies constituted the Iran Council of Churches through which they participated together for a number of years in the

Interchurch Literature Committee, the Interchurch Correspondence
Course, a radio ministry, a youth program, and a joint parish work in
the Khuzestan Church Council.

C. The Diocese of Egypt

Anglican work in **Egypt** was resumed in 1882 under the direction of CMS missionaries. W. H. Temple Gairdner (1873-1928), a
noted Arabist, organized the first small Anglican congregation in that
country. It was composed mainly of converts from Islam because of
Gairdner's refusal to proselytize from other Christian churches.
Today there are no more than one thousand Anglicans in Egypt, half
of them expatriates. Four Arabic-speaking congregations are in Cairo
and suburbs, each with its own pastor. English-speaking congregations are in Cairo and Alexandria with CMS chaplains, and in Port
Said led by a lay reader.[40]
Anglicans in Egypt regard their distinctive mission to be that
of a "bridge" church between Orthodox and Evangelical communities,
and of dialogue with Muslims. The latter objective was most vigorously pursued in Temple Gairdner's lifetime and, more recently,
during Bishop Kenneth Cragg's tenure in the 1970s.
In **Libya** the three hundred Anglicans are all expatriates,
mainly British and American.[41] The church building in Tripoli belonging to the Anglicans for many years was taken by the Libyan
government in the early 1970s for use in connection with a military
installation. That congregation has since used the building of an
interdenominational Union Church. Services are also held periodi-
cally in seven other centers: Benghazi, Misurata, Mersa, Bregha,
Beida, Tobruk, Abu Kamash, and Sebha.
In **Tunisia**, St. George's Anglican Church has been in the
capital city of Tunis for nearly a century. The 150 members of the
present congregation are expatriates from various national and ecclesiastical backgrounds, many of them non-Anglican.
The Anglican congregation in Algiers, the capital of **Algeria**,
is the westernmost constituent of the Diocese of Egypt.[42] It has an
estimated total constituency of three hundred.
The few Anglicans in **Somalia**—not more than 150 in total—
are in Mogadishu and Hargeisa. Those in Mogadishu (formerly a part
of Italian Somaliland) share the use of the Roman Catholic cathedral
and have a part-time pastor. The congregation is mainly expatriate,

but a few Somali Christians participate. The latter are the vestige of Moravian missionary activity in the early part of this century. Hargeisa in the north (formerly part of British Somaliland) has an Anglican church building, but the small congregation there depends entirely upon lay leadership.

D. The Diocese of Cyprus and the Gulf

About 850 people belong to four established parishes in Cyprus:[43] St. Paul's in Nicosia (the cathedral church), St. Helena's in Larnaca, St. Barnabas in Limassol, and St. Andrew's in Kyrenia, all with their own church buildings and resident chaplains. The Kyrenia parish is, since 1974, within the Turkish sector of the Island. Anglicans have regularly provided leadership in various interchurch affairs, including initial efforts to establish an ecumenical conference center at Aiya Napa.[44]

Of more than three thousand British residents in Kuwait, about half are involved in Anglican church activities. St. Paul's Church in Ahmadi is their only organized parish, and the church building there is made available to three or four Indian groups of diverse ecclesiastical backgrounds as well. Among the latter is a small congregation of the Church of South India, a denomination with which Anglicans have been in full communion since 1947.

In Bahrain about one thousand people, mainly British, participate in the Anglican Church—four hundred of them in Manama and the rest in Awali and elsewhere. The very beautiful parish church building in Manama was designed by the Rev. R. N. Sharp, a talented architect who also built the well-known church of St. Simon the Zealot in Shiraz, Iran. It is used by various Christian Indian groups as well as the Anglican congregation. St. Christopher's School on the same large compound has a student body of more than six hundred, including children of the royal family.

In the capital city of Qatar, the congregation of about 350 calls itself "Anglican and Allied Churches in Doha." It is in effect a community church composed of Europeans from all non-Catholic denominations. There are some Indian members as well as Europeans, and some Arab Anglicans and Protestants mainly from Lebanon and Palestine.

St. Andrew's Church in Abu Dhabi, like the church in Doha described above, is in fact a community church open to all but following the Anglican tradition in worship. In addition to an English-speaking congregation of about eight hundred members, its building is used by a variety of other groups: Mar Thomite, Indian Pentecostal, Indian Brethren, and others. The Anglican priest in Abu Dhabi is archdeacon, with responsibilities in the Gulf area as a whole.

In **Dubai** the Anglican-Community Church of about six hundred members has an even more multidenominational character than those in the Sultanates and Emirates to the north, although it is officially part of the Anglican diocese. Recent pastors have devoted considerable time in a ministry to seamen, because hundreds of ships call at the busy Dubai port throughout the year.

The few Anglicans in **Oman**, all expatriates, have been incorporated into an English-speaking congregation in Muscat, established by the mission of the Reformed Church in America. This congregation does not follow Anglican traditions or liturgical patterns as such, nor is it organically part of the Anglican diocese, but its pastor is "accredited" by that diocese to minister to the Anglicans in Oman.

Three other countries in the region have Anglican communities not under the jurisdiction of the Province of the Episcopal Church in Jerusalem and the Middle East: Morocco, Turkey, and Sudan.

Anglicans in **Morocco** belong to the Diocese of Gibraltar. A small congregation of about 150, mainly British and Americans, constitute the parish church of St. John the Evangelist in Casablanca.

Few Anglicans are any longer in **Turkey**. A chaplain is attached to the British Embassy in Ankara, but his ministry is virtually confined to his fellow countrymen in diplomatic service or educational institutions in that city. In Istanbul a large Anglican church building is adjacent to the British Consulate, recalling Ottoman days when a very substantial British community was there. The church building is now used only for special occasions three or four times each year. On ordinary Sundays the resident Anglican priest conducts services at a small chapel elsewhere in the city or at the Consulate.

In **Sudan** the Province of the Episcopal Church[45] has a total membership of more than 250,000 in four dioceses, a numerical strength exceeded only by that of the Roman Catholics in this country. However, over ninety-five percent of that total in both churches are Black African Sudanese of the southern provinces. This is a dramatic illustration of rapid Christian expansion among primal peoples compared with the very slow growth of churches in all Muslim areas.

Six northern Sudanese pastors serve the two thousand Arabic-speaking members of Anglican parishes in Khartoum, Omdurman,

Port Sudan, Wad Medani, and El Obeid. The church-related primary-intermediate school and high school in Khartoum, and a hospital and high school in Omdurman are all Sudanese directed with some CMS missionary personnel still on the staff.

All Saints Cathedral in Khartoum is an impressive monument to a time half a century ago when a large British community in Sudan was on a wave of optimism about their future there. That community has steadily declined since the 1950s. However, there are still enough Anglicans in Khartoum along with the Arabic-speaking congregation there to maintain a lively parish program. During the sixteen years of civil war in Sudan (1958-1974) this large cathedral was once again used to capacity by hundreds of tribal Christians from southern Sudan and Nubia who came as refugees to the capital city.

Three bishoprics in the southern provinces of Sudan together have a quarter of a million members in twenty-one organized parishes with several hundred outposts. The major centers are Juba, Maridi, Ibba, Yambio, Nzara, Bafuka, Lainga, Boken, Yei, Panyana, Angobi, Kajo Kazi, Rumbek, Tonj, Wau, Panekar, Akot, Bor, Lui, Mindri, and Malakal. Some, perhaps most, of the sixty indigenous pastors serving this enormous area were in exile during the civil war. Throughout those troubled years, the burden of pastoral care fell to lay catechists, and many of the church-related village schools had to be abandoned. Bishop Gwynne College, a joint Anglican-Presbyterian training center and the only school offering basic theological education, was closed. When the political situation began to stabilize in 1974, thousands who had fled either into northern Sudan or across the borders of neighboring African states returned to begin the long, hard task of rebuilding their homes, churches, and schools. But by 1982 normal activities in these southern provinces were again badly disrupted, and the fruit of Anglican missionary dedication since 1899 faces an uncertain future.

VII. The Protestant Churches

Protestant denominations and a wide variety of nondenominational and independent bodies are the result of missionary endeavor in the Middle East beginning early in the nineteenth century. Except in southern Sudan and Egypt they have a relatively small membership. Those two facts, that the indigenous Protestant churches are of

71

comparatively recent origin and that they are a minority within a minority makes their contribution to the region even more remarkable. The significance of their educational, medical, and welfare services is quite out of proportion to the size of the Protestant community. In some endeavors, notably Bible translation and distribution, mass communications, and higher education for women, they have been pioneers. Important universities, colleges, secondary schools, and medical centers in the area (some of which no longer retain a specific church identification in name or administration) are the products of mission agencies that brought the Protestant churches into existence. Most of these institutions are now under the auspices of the churches themselves or of independent boards of directors.

Protestant churches also minister, as do Anglicans and Latin-rite Catholics, through a number of congregations composed mainly or entirely of expatriates. Major cities of the area such as Cairo and Istanbul have nondenominational community churches affiliated with the Committee on Overseas Union Churches of the National Council of the Churches of Christ in the U.S.A. Other such English-language congregations throughout the area are under denominational or independent auspices. French-speaking and German-speaking Protestants have their own church organizations. These congregations of foreign constituency generally have no organic relationship to the churches of entirely indigenous membership, but several of them are involved in the life of the respective countries in genuinely ecumenical ways.

Two generalizations can be made about Protestant churches in the Middle East as a whole: (1) Nowhere in the area are they older than the first quarter of the nineteenth century. (2) The vast majority of their membership came originally from Orthodox and Eastern-rite Catholic churches. This has left a residue of mutual suspicion and ill will that can be overcome only by more creative ecumenical relationships than yet exist, especially between Protestant and Orthodox churches.

In foregoing sections I have described the Latin-rite Catholic and Anglican constituencies country-by-country. It seems more meaningful to introduce the Protestant churches according to the categories of their ecclesiastical heritage, and in an alphabetical arrangement.[46.]

A. *Baptist Churches*

Baptist churches in the Middle East, with a wide variety of missionary origins, have a small but growing membership.

Those related to the mission board of the Southern Baptist Convention (U.S.A.) are located primarily in Israel and the West Bank, Jordan, and Lebanon, with smaller groups in Egypt, Algeria, and elsewhere. A regional director of the mission resides in Nicosia, Cyprus. This Baptist agency maintains a missionary force of nearly one hundred Americans in Israel, Jordan, Lebanon, and North Yemen alone. The indigenous congregations in Israel and the West Bank have a total membership of only 250, but the vigorous Baptist work there includes two bookstores, a school, four training centers, an orphanage and farm, a publications office, and a hospital (in Gaza). In Jordan there are five congregations with a total of three hundred members, along with five schools and a hospital. In Lebanon their six hundred members form fifteen congregations and groups. There they maintain two secondary schools, a theological seminary and radio ministry at Mansourieh, and a campus center adjacent to the American University of Beirut. Congregations of expatriate American Southern Baptists are in Jerusalem, Ankara, and Saudi Arabia.

The Conservative Baptist Church (U.S.A.) sponsors four small congregations and a school in Jordan. Throughout the region there are other Baptist groups with a combined membership of about two thousand. Some consist of no more than one or two congregations each, but they maintain student centers, Bible schools, and correspondence courses of their own. These include the Bible Baptist Church, the Baptist Bible Fellowship, the Evangelical Baptist Church, and others.

Many of the independent missionaries in the Middle East are affiliated with various Baptist congregations in their respective homelands. Baptist personnel, both foreign and local, also have a significant role in nondenominational mission groups and agencies throughout the area, such as the Sudan Interior Mission, the North Africa Mission (now called Arab World Ministries), the Gospel Missionary Union, the Worldwide Evangelization Crusade, Operation Mobilization, Campus Crusade, Youth for Christ, BMMF Interserve, and Youth with a Mission.

B. *Lutheran Churches*

Apart from their long-established work in Jerusalem and the West Bank, Lutherans constitute a very small part of the total Protestant community in the Middle East. Lutheran missions from Europe and America have instead concentrated on East Africa and Ethiopia where indigenous churches of the Lutheran tradition are large and

73

influential.

The Evangelical Lutheran Church of Jordan, dating from German missionary endeavors in 1860, now has a total of about thirteen hundred members in five congregations served by Palestinian pastors: Jerusalem, Beit Jala, Bethlehem, Beit Sahour, and Ramallah on the West Bank. Another congregation of about fifty is in Amman, Jordan. The impressive building of the Church of the Redeemer in East Jerusalem accommodates both German- and Arabic-speaking congregations. A large secondary school is nearby, and the German Evangelical Institute for Archaeological Research is also in Jerusalem.

The Schneller Schools, one near Amman and the other in Lebanon's Bekaa Valley, have long rendered notable service in agricultural and mechanical training. Both institutions are directed by a German Lutheran society.

A Norwegian Lutheran mission serves about one hundred Jewish Christians in Haifa and Jaffa, and there is a Scandinavian Seamen's Mission at the ports of Haifa and Ashdod.

One or two tiny congregations in the Kurdish area of northern Iraq were established by the Lutheran Orient Mission.

The Middle East Lutheran Ministry with headquarters in Beirut is sponsored by the Missouri Synod, U.S.A. This organization does not seek to establish churches as such, but rather serves the total Christian community in a variety of ways.

C. Methodist Church of North Africa (now Eglise Protestante en Algérie)

The Methodist Church of North Africa was located in Algeria, almost exclusively in the eastern part of that country around Oran and Constantine. This small community of about 350 native Algerian members, with another twenty across the border in Tunisia, was an outgrowth of work done since the latter part of the nineteenth century by Methodist missionaries from the United States. In 1972 the Methodist Church of North Africa merged with the French Reformed Church in Algeria (an entirely expatriate membership of 850) and a tiny group of Mennonites. The united body is called Eglise Protestante en Algérie.

D. Presbyterian and Reformed Churches

Because of early nineteenth-century missionary initiatives, the Presbyterian and Reformed churches together comprise the largest

Aleppo, Syria. Syrian Orthodox Archbishop and priest.
Photo: Norman Horner.

Inside Old Syrian Orthodox Cathedral, Mardin, Turkey.

Hermit monks' caves, Deir Zafaran Monastery near Mardin, Turkey.
Photo: Norman Horner.

Kitchen, Deir Zafaran Monastery, near Mardin, Turkey (Syrian Orthodox).
Photo: Norman Horner.

Deir Zafaran Monastery, near Mardin, Turkey (Syrian Orthodox).
Photo: Norman Horner.

Soviet Armenia, Echmiadzin Cathedral. Priest blessing animal offerings.
Photo: Norman Horner.

Armenian Orthodox liturgy, Teheran, Iran. Photo: Sherman Fung.

Armenian Orthodox, Teheran, Iran. Footwashing ceremony during Holy Week. Photo: Sherman Fung.

Armenian Orthodox Feast of St. Gregory, Antelias, Lebanon,
Catholicosate. Photo: Norman Horner.

Near Bikfaya. Maronite Church, Lebanon. Photo: Norman Horner.

Assyrian (Nestorian) Liturgy. Priest reading from Liturgy of the Apostles, Teheran, Iran. Photo: Sherman Fung.

Assyrian (Nestorian) Teheran, Iran. Old man receiving communion. Photo: Sherman Fung.

Greek Orthodox, Teheran, Iran. Easter vigil, serving communion to young boy. Photo: Sherman Fung.

Greek Orthodox Teheran, Iran. Good Friday services, carrying epitaphion (symbolic body of Christ). Photo: Sherman Fung.

and most widespread Protestant community in the region.

1. The Union of Armenian Evangelical Churches in the Near East is an outgrowth of a reformation movement in the Armenian Apostolic Church and work begun 160 years ago by the American Board of Commissioners for Foreign Missions (originally Congregational and Presbyterian, later exclusively Congregational). The first Armenian Evangelical congregation was established in Constantinople (now Istanbul) in 1846. Until the massacres in Turkey at the turn of the present century, the number of Armenian Protestants in that country alone reached a total of forty-two thousand with some ninety ordained pastors.[47] By 1920, however, their numbers were greatly reduced by death and dispersion.

The Union has long been entirely autonomous. Nine congregations in Lebanon, with a total membership of about five thousand, are concentrated in Beirut and in the solidly Armenian enclave around Anjar near the Syrian border. Another five thousand are in Syria where the largest of their twelve congregations are in Aleppo and around Kessab in the western part of the country. Smaller groups are in Istanbul and eastern Turkey, Egypt, Iran, and Iraq.

The vast Armenian diaspora in Europe, the United States, and Australia includes at least ten thousand Protestants who have organized their own schools, congregations, and welfare agencies.

Armenian Evangelical churches in the Middle East have a distinguished record in educational work. In Beirut, for example, their schools still educate about one-fifth of the total Armenian primary and secondary school population, although these Protestants represent less than four percent of the Armenians in that city. They also maintain the only Armenian school of higher education in the region, Haigazian College, also in Beirut. Aleppo College, an influential secondary school in Syria, is under joint auspices of the Armenian Evangelical Union and the Arabic-speaking National Evangelical Synod of Syria and Lebanon.

2. The Coptic Evangelical Church is by far the largest Protestant church in Egypt and in many respects the strongest Protestant denomination in the Middle East. It is the outgrowth of work begun in 1853 by United Presbyterian missionaries from the U.S.A. For many years it was part of the General Assembly of that American church, but it has been fully autonomous since 1958. Structured as the Synod of the Nile with eight geographical presbyteries throughout the country, this church has two hundred established congregations and fifty outposts. The adult communicant membership is about thirty thousand and the total constituency is estimated at one hundred thousand. The church has 180 ordained Egyptian pastors and twenty licensed lay evangelists, a staff large enough not only to care for the congregations in Egypt but also to provide pastors for several non-Egyptian Arab congregations in Iraq, the Arabian Gulf States, and Sudan. The Coptic Evangelical Seminary in Cairo trains pastors for this church and for some of the other evangelical bodies in Egypt. Evening classes for the laity and an institute for Christian-Muslim relations are included in the seminary's program.

Nineteen primary-secondary schools were inherited from the American mission including a prestigious college preparatory school, Ramses College for Girls in Cairo. About fifty other primary schools are maintained by parishes in both upper and lower Egypt. The synod sponsors the Emmanuel Leadership Training Center in Cairo and two student centers in Assuit and Cairo. An audio-visual center in Cairo is affiliated with the Middle East Council of Churches, an ecumenical organization in which the Coptic Evangelicals play an important role.

The Coptic Evangelical Organization for Social Services (CEOSS) conducts a widespread program of literacy, adult education, family planning, child and health care, agricultural self-help projects, and leadership development among women. CEOSS serves a total of fifty-five villages throughout the country. This church also shares responsibility with personnel of the American Presbyterians mission for a hospital at Tanta.

3. The Evangelical Church of Iran was first established in 1855, the outgrowth of an American Presbyterian mission that began work in that country twenty years earlier. Three presbyteries were organized in 1933 and redistributed along linguistic rather than geographical lines in 1971. The membership of the church is fifty-five percent Assyrian, twenty-one percent Armenian, and twenty-four percent Persian and Jewish. Eighteen congregations, led by seven ordained pastors and several lay evangelists, have a total membership of about three thousand and are widely distributed across the northern half of the country. A synod consisting of both lay and ordained representatives was formed in 1934, its central office located in Teheran.

This church has historical relationships with a school for practical nurses at Mashed and the Community School in Teheran, both closed since the 1979 revolution in Iran, and with Damavand

College for women in the same city, now renamed and controlled by the new government of the country. A very promising center for leadership training in Teheran was also terminated in 1979. Six church related elementary schools are presumably continuing.

4. The Evangelical Church of Sudan is found exclusively in the Arabic-speaking northern part of that country. It began as a presbytery of the Coptic Evangelical Church under the guidance of American Presbyterian missionaries in 1900, but has long been an autonomous organization. A total of about six hundred members belong to eight congregations in Khartoum, Omdurman, Khartoum North, Atbara, Port Sudan, Gadaref, Wad Medani, Kosti, and El Obeid. The six pastors are Egyptians, trained at the Coptic Evangelical Seminary in Cairo. During the years of civil war in Sudan (1958-1974) these pastors also ministered to large numbers of southern Sudanese refugees in several of the cities and towns named above.

With no missionary personnel at present, this church maintains six elementary and intermediate schools, a commercial high school, a children's home, a literature center in Khartoum, and a literacy program among women. It also has a training school for lay evangelists at the Gereif Conference Center near Khartoum. The Evangelical Church of Sudan is a member of both the Sudan Church Council and the Middle East Council of Churches. For some time it has been in process of negotiations toward union with the much larger Sudanese Church of Christ in the Nubian mountains.

5. The National Evangelical Synod of Syria and Lebanon arose from the work begun in 1823 by the American Board of Commissioners for Foreign Missions and transferred to the Presbyterian Church, U.S.A. in 1870. Arabic-speaking congregations formed a synod with three presbyteries in 1920. The presbyteries were dissolved in 1932, but the synod structure has been maintained, with headquarters in Beirut. Since 1958 this church has had full responsibility for institutional work of various kinds begun by the sponsoring missions.

There are now about four thousand adult communicants, and the church claims a total constituency of twenty thousand in the two countries. Its forty organized congregations, along with some twenty other informal groups, are served by twenty-two ordained pastors and five lay preachers. Two hospitals, one in Lebanon and one in Syria, are directly related to the synod. Its twelve elementary and eight secondary schools include such institutions as Aleppo College (managed jointly with the Armenian Evangelical Union) and the Beirut Evangelical School for Girls. Beirut College for Women (now the coeducational Beirut University College), first women's college in the Middle East and still one of the region's most important schools, has a direct relationship to the National Evangelical Synod. Ties with the American University of Beirut are now merely historical and nominal, yet that great institution also began as part of the same Presbyterian enterprise. The National Evangelical Synod is a member of the Middle East Council of Churches, and a constituent of the Near East School of Theology which serves as the advanced training center for its clergy.

6. The National Evangelical Church in Beirut has common origin with the National Evangelical Synod of Syria and Lebanon described immediately above. It consists of one large parish in Beirut and two smaller congregations in Lebanese villages, with a total constituency of about twenty-five hundred. Arguments concerning property control and representation led these three congregations to form an association independent of the synod in the early 1950s. Reunion was considered but not implemented in 1958, and the National Evangelical Church remains an autonomous body. This church maintains two primary-secondary schools. It is informally related to an Arab evangelical congregation in Damascus, and both groups are again negotiating a reunion with the Evangelical Synod.

7. The Presbyterian Church in the Sudan dates from American missionary work among the tribal peoples of the southern provinces beginning in 1902. In 1948 it was made a presbytery of the Synod of the Nile (Coptic Evangelical Church, Egypt) and it became the independent Church of Christ in the Upper Nile in 1956. That name was later changed to Presbyterian Church in the Sudan. Close association is maintained with the Evangelical Church of Sudan (see description above), looking toward the ultimate formation of a single Presbyterian synod in the country as a whole.

This church has a total membership of about three thousand. There are twelve organized congregations: Malakal United Church (jointly Presbyterian-Episcopal), Doleib Hill, Nasir, Abwong, Fangak, Akobo, Pibo, Ler, Kodok, Melmut, and Bentiu. These include outposts in some thirty other villages, and they are served by eight ordained ministers and a number of lay catechists.

The church maintains a number of primary schools in towns

and villages, and a bookshop in Malakal. Through the Sudan Evangelical Council the Presbyterian Church in the Sudan has close relationships with the much larger Episcopal Church also in the southern provinces. Together the two churches control Bishop Gwynne Theological College for training pastors. Clergy of both churches receive more advanced training at the Near East School of Theology in Beirut and at St. Paul's Theological College in Limuru, Kenya.

8. In several countries of the Middle East there are congregations of the Presbyterian and Reformed family whose circumstances oblige them to function more or less independently and in isolation from the larger associations.

The three Arab Evangelical congregations in **Iraq** are at Baghdad, Kirkuk, and Basra, all served by Egyptian pastors sent from the Coptic Evangelical Church. Assyrian Evangelical groups in both Baghdad and Basra are currently without ordained clergy.

Three Arabic-speaking congregations in the Arabian Gulf States are related to the long and significant ministry of the Reformed Church in America. The building of the Evangelical Church of **Kuwait** is used by such a variety of groups throughout the week as to require a very precise hour-by-hour schedule. Among them is a congregation of people who immigrated years ago from Turkey, now led by an Egyptian pastor. In **Bahrain** the Arabic-speaking segment of the Evangelical Church, also served by an Egyptian pastor, consists largely of people reared as Christians in orphanages of the Reformed Church mission. A smaller group in **Oman** (Muscat) is still led by a missionary pastor.

In **Israel** the Overseas Board of the Church of Scotland has three congregations with a total of about two hundred members in Jerusalem, Jaffa, and Tiberias. That mission also maintains a school, clinic, and hostel. A hospital in Nazareth under the auspices of the Edinburgh Medical Missionary Society includes a program of nurses' training. The Independent Board for Presbyterian Foreign Missions (Bible Presbyterian Church, U.S.A.) has a school, hospital, and one small congregation of local people in Bethlehem on the West Bank.

A tiny Greek Evangelical group in **Cyprus** was recently joined by a handful of Greek and Armenian Cypriots formerly related to the work of the Reformed Presbyterian Mission from the U.S.A. That mission was discontinued in the late 1970s, but the two American Academies (secondary schools) they formerly operated in Nicosia and Larnaca continue independently under the same names.

E. Other Denominational and Non-denominational Churches

This category includes a rather vast proliferation of congregations throughout the region, established by conservative-evangelical denominations, nondenominational missions, and independent missionaries. The following summary is admittedly incomplete. It is merely an attempt to list those at work in more than one country, more or less in the order of their numerical strength.

The Assemblies of God, a North American Pentecostal denomination, claims a membership of about eleven thousand in **Egypt**, where their missionaries have organized a total of one hundred forty-four groups throughout the country. A large nondenominational orphanage in Assuit looks to this church for leadership in administration and financial support. In **Iran**, a total of two thousand people in nine congregations called the Assyrian Assemblies, and sixteen known as the Filadelfia Assemblies (largely Armenians) are the outgrowth of Assemblies of God mission effort. Much smaller groupings of this affiliation are in **Lebanon**, **Jordan**, and **Israel**.

Plymouth Brethren, known in the Middle East as Christian Brethren, are difficult to number because of the informal structure of their fellowship groups. They do, however, have a significant total throughout the region. They are most numerous in **Egypt** where six thousand is not an unrealistic estimate, and another six hundred in **Israel**, **Turkey**, **Iran**, and **Cyprus** combined. Largely or entirely expatriate groups of Christian Brethren are in **Tunisia, Morocco, Saudi Arabia, Kuwait**, and **South Yemen**.

The Free Methodist Church of North America through its General Mission Board has a thriving work in **Egypt**. An estimated thirty-five hundred members are in some seventy congregations of about fifty people each. That mission agency is not represented elsewhere in the region, but it is here listed because of its relative numerical importance to Egyptian Protestantism.

The Seventh-Day Adventist Middle East Division reports a total of thirty-five churches with an aggregate membership of 2,275. The majority of them are in **Egypt** and **Lebanon**, with smaller congregations in **Iraq, Iran, Israel, Jordan,** and southern **Sudan.** Adventist groups of only about fifteen people each are in **Cyprus** and **Turkey.**

Under direction of the church's North Africa Union, congregations of no more than fifty (mainly expatriates) in each country are found in Algeria, Libya, Morocco, and Tunisia.

The Middle East Division of this church coordinates the work of five secondary schools (in Egypt, Jordan, and Lebanon), Middle East College and the Middle East Press (in Lebanon), two food processing plants (in Egypt and Lebanon), two orphanages (in Egypt and Jordan), and six correspondence course programs (in Cyprus, Iran, Iraq, Jordan, Lebanon, and Turkey). Seventh-Day Adventists are well known for their hospitals in other parts of the world, but those they established in the Middle East no longer exist under their auspices.

The Church in East Central Sudan began in 1937 as an outgrowth of the Sudan Interior Mission's much older work in the great African expanse known as the Sudanic belt. This church now has a membership of fourteen hundred in some fourteen congregations.

The Church of God (headquarters in Anderson, Indiana, U.S.A.) has three congregations in **Lebanon** with a total of five hundred members, and two in northern **Syria** with about one hundred each. In **Egypt** the fifteen groups related to this mission have a combined membership of no more than five hundred, but the church maintains a bookshop and publishes a periodical magazine there. An extensive program of evangelism among youth is a special emphasis of this church in all three countries.

The Evangelical Christian Alliance Church is the fruit of work done in the Middle East by the Christian and Missionary Alliance, U.S.A. The combined membership of about nine hundred represents a total of some twenty groups and organized congregations in **Jordan, Syria, Lebanon,** and **Israel.** Those in Israel are largely expatriates belonging to the International Alliance Church in Jerusalem, but a small group is in Beersheba. About half the members in Lebanon were also temporary residents from overseas. In Beirut this church had a Bible training school, a fellowship of university students, a program of theological education by extension, and a youth center until these activities were interrupted by the civil war.

The Church of the Nazarene, with some twenty small groups and organized congregations, has a total membership of about 650 in **Jordan, Lebanon, Syria,** and **Israel.** Three schools (two in Jordan and one in Lebanon) are related to this church.

The Churches of Christ, U.S.A., began missionary activities in **Lebanon** in 1961. Three congregations with a total of about 100 members were organized in that country, along with a Bible training school in Beirut. A program of literature distribution and a correspondence course that extended to Egypt, Syria, and Jordan was maintained until interrupted by the war in Lebanon. In **Israel** their membership of two hundred consists of a largely expatriate congregation in West Jerusalem and two small indigenous groups in Nazareth and Eilabun (Galilee). A secondary school at Eilabun includes pupils from several surrounding villages.

The Church of God of Prophecy, a North American Pentecostal body with headquarters in Cleveland, Tennessee, began a mission to **Cyprus** in 1935. Their only church building is in the outskirts of Nicosia, but cell groups meet in several other towns and cities in the homes of the members. With a communicant membership of only 150, this church is nevertheless the only Protestant community in the country with exclusively Greek-Cypriot constituency. In 1965 the Church of God began a mission in **Israel.** Three small congregations with a combined membership of about two hundred are now in that country.

The Armenian Evangelical Spiritual Brotherhood began in Aleppo, Syria, in 1920 as an association of people who withdrew from other Armenian churches (Evangelical, Catholic, and Orthodox) to emphasize a close-knit and pietistic way of life. Lay leadership is a central concept of the Armenian Brethren, and they have no ordained ministry. Small groups with a total of about 325 members are now found in **Lebanon, Syria, Egypt, Iraq,** and **Iran.**

A complete listing of every Protestant congregation, independent church group, and para-church organization in the Middle East might be possible to compile, but only after an inordinate expenditure of time and effort, and for this particular study it would have dubious value. The churches and fellowship groups listed above are the most widely known and are represented in more than one country of the region, but a proliferation of other Pentecostal, independent, and sectarian groups is to be found in most countries throughout the area.

THE CHURCHES IN TODAY'S REGION-WIDE TURMOIL

The involvement of Christians in the wider social and religious life of the Middle East is different from one section to another, but a few generalizations are possible. Christians are minorities in their respective countries everywhere apart from Cyprus, and politically powerless minorities except in Lebanon. Yet their social influence is quite disproportionate to their numbers. By and large they are better educated than the Muslim majority, and hence prominent Christian doctors, teachers, journalists, lawyers, bankers, artists, and other professional leaders are found even where the percentage of Christians in the overall population is negligible. In general the Christians are economically middle class. There are poor people among them, but hardly anywhere are they the poorest of the poor. And Christians, no less than Muslims, feel the currents of political upheaval. They are victims, but also in some cases perpetrators, of the unrest that has now led to chaos in much of the region and utter disaster in some parts of it during the past fifteen years.

The following is a brief summary of the Christian situation in each of three major segments of the region: (1) the Arab East, geographically including Israel, (2) Libya and the North African Maghrib or Arab West, and (3) the non-Arab countries—Turkey, Cyprus, and Iran.

I. The Arab East

The vast majority of Middle Eastern Christians live in the Arabic-speaking Fertile Crescent, from Egypt northward and eastward through Israel and the occupied West Bank, Jordan, Lebanon, Syria, and Iraq. Since the end of the Second World War no date is more decisive in the modern history of this part of the region than 1948. In that year the emergence of Israel as a sovereign state with military power and territorial ambitions began a chain of events that has revived ancient antagonisms and introduced new rivalries. Religious minorities and governments alike have been confronted with problems that have no visible solution. With consequent hardening of Arab nationalism and a revival of Islamic fundamentalism, there is a renewed tendency to use the word "Arab" synonymously with "Muslim" rather than in its proper reference to anyone whose native language is Arabic.

Egypt. The Islamic revival has been easily exploited by popular and often charismatic leaders in Egypt, the homeland of more Christians than are in all other parts of the Middle East combined. Until the early 1950s Christians in that country had been represented in government somewhat beyond their numbers in the overall population. But with the emergence of Jamal Abdul Nasser the policy became more restrictive, only a very few government posts of secondary importance being granted to Christians. Nasser's successors to date, Anwar Sadat and Hosni Mubaraq, have made no further concessions.

This is not to suggest that the present Egyptian government is anti-Christian as such. I have already evaluated the recent restrictions on Coptic Pope Shenooda III as a balancing act to avoid increasing outbursts from Muslim extremists who had made vilifying charges against him (see the section on the Coptic Orthodox Church, above). I believe, moreover, that increasingly restrictive policies in some other Arab states in recent years may be similarly explained. The zeal of the recent Iranian revolution could be easily exported to the Muslim world at large, and the Arab governments have reason to fear it. The Islamic fundamentalism of Arab leader Qaddafi in Libya is scarcely less threatening to political stability in the countries with moderate regimes.

Most regrettably, however, the long-time Coptic Orthodox initiatives for better Christian-Muslim relationships have reached a virtual impasse. This gives added urgency to Catholic and Protestant efforts in that direction. The precarious interfaith balance that now exists in Egypt could be upset by even minor provocations from either side.

Israel and the Occupied West Bank. Christians continue to emigrate from Israel and the occupied territories. This is not because they are singled out for harsh treatment; in that respect they fare better than their Muslim neighbors. It is because the majority of them are Palestinians who share with Palestinian Muslims a deep resentment of Israeli rule and the indignities of second-class citizenship in their own homeland.

Emigration has for some time threatened to reduce Jerusalem to a museum of Christian history rather than the center of a living Christian community. There were forty-five thousand Christians of all confessions in the Old City and environs in 1947. By 1979 their number had declined to ten thousand and they continue to leave.[48]

For obvious political and financial reasons the Israeli government seeks the approval of Christian churches, both within and outside Israel, for the Zionist cause. However, with the exception of the Maronites, the traditional churches throughout the Middle East deplore Zionism as fervently as do the Muslims. Nor has any support for it come from the Vatican or from ecumenical Protestant councils in the West. The Israelis therefore curry the favor of groups known to view modern political Israel as the fulfillment of biblical prophecy.

Paradoxically, some of the Christian groups most ardently courted by the Israeli establishment for political reasons are also viewed by Israelis as a serious threat to Jewish religious solidarity. There are now an estimated two thousand "Messianic Jews" in Israel, converts to Christianity and associated mainly with the conservative-evangelical missions. Under pressure from the radical Agudat Israel party, the Knesset (parliament) passed legislation in 1977 prohibiting the use of any enticements to change religious affiliation. This, according to local evangelical Christians, was intended as an "anti-missionary" law. But "it was obviously recognized by Rabbi Abromowitz and his colleagues [in the Knesset] that a law outlawing all missionary work in Israel would encounter too much pressure both inside and outside Israel and cost the country many of its evangelical supporters."[49]

Christian-Muslim relationships seem to be more relaxed in Israel and the West Bank than elsewhere in the Middle East. This is probably because Christians share with Muslims a second-class citizenship and a common desire for Palestinian autonomy.

Jordan. Christians enjoy more economic and social opportunity in the Hashemite Kingdom of Jordan than elsewhere in the Middle East except Lebanon and Cyprus. Although they constitute less than ten percent of the total population, they have a disproportionately large representation in the Jordanian parliament and hold important government portfolios, ambassadorial appointments abroad, and positions of military rank.[50] Most Christians in Jordan are of Palestinian origin (as is at least half the Muslim population of the country)[51] and even those coming as refugees from the Israeli-Palestinian conflict since 1948 have been reasonably well absorbed into Jordanian society. There are no Christians in the large camps maintained by the United Nations Relief and Works Agency for Palestine Refugees in the Near East (UNRWA).

Christian numbers, and consequently influence, have grown in recent years by reason of further immigration from the occupied West Bank. As a result, the Orthodox Patriarchate of Jerusalem now has a larger constituency in Jordan than in all the areas under Israeli rule. Unfortunately, however, this church with over fifty percent of all Jordanian Christians in its membership now maintains no schools above primary level in the country, and its parish clergy are poorly educated. Christian impact on the social and political life of Jordan is therefore increasingly Catholic and to some extent Anglican, largely because of their prestigious schools and influential clergy.

Lebanon. At the time of Lebanese independence in 1943, Christians and Muslims were in approximately equal numbers. The Christians in fact had a very slight majority but a much larger advantage in terms of political, economic, and military power. Today the numerical strength is clearly on the Muslim side (about 60/40).[52] Forty percent is still a much higher ratio of Christians in the total population than is found in any other Arab state. For good or ill they still insist on holding the balance of power in Lebanon. But the question is no longer whether they can retain that power in an undivided country, but whether or not permanent division into separate Christian and Muslim states is inevitable.

As of this writing the political future of Lebanon remains so uncertain that any predictions are risky. It seems clear, however, that if the unique Lebanese experiment of Christian-Muslim political cooperation is to survive, representation of the various religious communities will have to be reapportioned to reflect the actual demographic situation. This is not simply a matter of curtailing Christian domination of the parliament and ministries. It must also reckon with the fact that the Shi'ite Muslims now outnumber the Sunnis. Thus the current Shi'ite unrest is caused no less by the intransigence of the Sunni Muslim establishment than by the Maronite Christians. A confessional system of government as such is not generally opposed by the Muslims. The experiment during the first forty years of the country's independence worked to the advantage of the Christians and Muslims alike in terms of economic prosperity and personal freedom. But Lebanon has tragically become the battleground for other nations whose political and religious designs it is helpless to control.

Syria. With no more than 850,000 Christians in total, Syria is nevertheless headquarters for three important churches in the

Middle East. The Antiochene Greek Orthodox, Syrian Orthodox, and Melkite patriarchs all reside in Damascus. The Christian population is concentrated in the coastal area around Latakia, in Aleppo, and in the eastern Jazira. Smaller but still considerable numbers of Christians are in Damascus.

Emigration was substantial in the 1960s, especially into Lebanon, but most of the Christian communities have remained fairly stable since then and have resumed a slow growth by natural increase. There is some migration of Christians from one part of the country to another. The Maronites in that country, for example, are mainly a subsistence agricultural people living in predominantly Christian villages of the Syrian littoral. Their youth in particular now tend to seek other kinds of employment in larger towns and villages.

Syrian Christians are prominent in the business and professional life of the country, and most of this elite are the products of church-related schools. In the early 1970s new regulations obliged all private schools to accept government appointed co-principals, to follow a curriculum designed by the government's ministry of education, to provide Islamic religious instruction for Muslim pupils, and to avoid the use of any names for schools that would identify them with a particular church. In consequence Maronite, Melkite, Syrian Catholic, and Latin-rite Catholic churches all decided to close their schools. Orthodox, Protestant, and all Armenian churches adjusted to the new demand and have kept theirs open to date, but not without sacrificing some of the prestige and educational excellence those schools formerly enjoyed.

Christian-Muslim relationships in Syria are surely not better, and perhaps even less cordial than in neighboring states. This is not reflected in open hostility, of which there has been little in recent years, but in the tendency of the Christian communities to be somewhat defensive and self-contained. Among the strong voices urging them to greater participation in the total life of the country is that of Neophytos Edelby, Melkite Archbishop of Aleppo. Edelby is probably the most widely respected and influential Christian leader in Aleppo. Through his writings and television appearances he has repeatedly called upon Arab Christians throughout the region to demonstrate their Arab identity by joining with others, irrespective of religious affiliation, in whatever promotes the welfare of their nations as a whole.

Iraq. With a population considerably larger than that of Syria, Iraq has less than half as many Christians. These are concentrated in three parts of the country: the Baghdad area (fifty-two percent), Mosul and surrounding villages in the north (thirty percent), and in the south around Basra (eighteen percent).[53] The fact that more than half the Christians now live in the vicinity of Baghdad is a fairly recent development. Before 1947 there was a much heavier concentration in the north,[54] but many thousands have since sought refuge and/or employment nearer the capital.

Emigration to other countries accounts for a marked reduction in the number of Christians of all communions who were in Iraq before 1947. Many have gone to Lebanon, seeking visas for ultimate residence in the Americas or Australia.[55] Often unable to get such visas a large number stayed on in Lebanon, temporarily or permanently increasing the membership of the Assyrian Church of the East in that country, and to some extent that of the Syrian Orthodox and Chaldean Catholic churches. Some of these "refugees" now face an unexpected problem. A more restrictive policy in Lebanon with regard to residence permits for all foreigners, and the intolerable living conditions resulting from the war, leaves them with an uncertain future.

The Iraqi government's increasingly nationalistic and anti-Western stance has resulted in the virtual elimination of Western missionary personnel from that country. American Jesuits had established Baghdad College (a secondary school) in the 1930s and Al-Hikma University in 1958. Two important secondary schools, for girls in Baghdad and for boys in Basra, were for a number of years under the auspices of the United Mission to Iraq, an American Protestant agency. Those institutions provided the finest general education available, but the Jesuits were expelled in 1968 and the foreign Protestant personnel in 1969. The government has not severed diplomatic relationships with the Vatican, but Iraqi Christians of all denominations are subject to suspicion for associations with Western church organizations.[56]

Freedom of religion is guaranteed by the Iraqi constitution. Since 1972 Syriac, along with Arabic, has been permitted as a medium of instruction in the primary and secondary schools Christian children attend. Iraqi Christians are well represented in business and professional life. Yet they have virtually no voice in political affairs, although the recent Iraq-Iran war may have brought Christians in both countries closer to their respective governments.

I. ARAB EAST: IRAQ, ARABIAN PENINSULA

The Arabian peninsula. Saudi Arabia along with thirteen autonomous sheikhdoms and emirates is not merely part of the Muslim world; it is the religious center of that world. The peninsula as a whole shares an Islamic conservatism that recognizes no other faith for the indigenous people. The number of truly "native" Christians is infinitesimal—less than150 along the Arabian gulf coast from Kuwait to Oman, and another four hundred or so in North and South Yemen. Christians in this area are therefore almost exclusively expatriates, but there are many thousands of them.[57] In several of the Gulf States (notably Kuwait, Qatar, Abu Dhabi, and Dubai) the number of foreigners greatly exceeds that of the native population. This accounts for a higher percentage of Christians in the total population than one would expect to find in such strongholds of very conservative Islam.

The impact of expatriate Christians on the life of the Arabian peninsula is quite different from that of the indigenous Christian communities who lived there in early centuries, but it is not inconsequential. The Muslim rulers in Kuwait, Abu Dhabi, Bahrain, and Oman have been particularly friendly to them, even making large personal donations to some of the church building funds. This good will probably reflects appreciation for earlier missionary contributions. Less than a generation ago, as one secular historian notes: "In Kuwait, as in Qatar and the Trucial States, such educational and health facilities as existed were largely provided by Christian missionaries, true pioneers in ecumenism who stayed on in Arabia to teach and heal even after discovering the impregnability of Muslim belief."[58]

The Arabian peninsula has undergone more rapid and far-reaching changes in economic and technological development during the last twenty-five years than almost anywhere else on earth. An accompanying "Westernization" of lifestyle of upper and middle classes in the society is a potential invitation to a strong reaction from Islamic fundamentalism, comparable to what has already happened in neighboring Iran. The relatively favorable position foreign Christians now enjoy should therefore not be taken for granted.

II. Libya and the North African Maghrib

The early church in the area now comprising Libya and the Maghrib (Arab West) was profoundly important to the Christian world at large, but it never became truly indigenous and had little impact on the Berber masses living outside the imported Roman culture. It was already in decline before the Muslim invasions began at the end of the seventh century, and by the fifteenth century it had virtually disappeared. The churches that flourished much later under French, Italian, and Spanish colonialism merely reintroduced European Christianity and failed to establish any deeper roots in the soil of the area than had their predecessors. Hence, with the rise of political independence and the expulsion of many thousands of Europeans in the 1960s, the remaining churches were once again decimated. Across North Africa today from the western border of Egypt to the Atlantic the Christian population is small and composed almost entirely of foreigners.[59]

In *Libya* Islam is as conservative as that of the Arabian peninsula, and President Qaddafi is the most influential guardian of Libyan conservatism. Press censorship and the almost total absence of foreign journals from the newsstands is as much to safeguard conventional morality as to prevent political subversion. The claim that "there is not a single Libyan Christian" is all but literally true within Libya itself, although some Libyan converts to Christianity (both Catholics and Protestants) are living abroad, mainly in southern Europe. Less than thirty-six thousand people, all expatriates and relatively few of them permanent residents of the country, are involved in the organized churches.

Tunisia is a more liberal Islamic society than Libya. The people now in political power are products of Seddika College where the mixture of French and Arabic culture is more conducive to religious tolerance. During his long tenure in office, now retired President Bourgiba approved a symbolic rather than literalistic observance of the Ramadan fast and interpreted *jihad* in the modern situation as primarily a war against poverty and illiteracy.

There are about thirty thousand Europeans now resident in the country, including two thousand French teachers in universities and secondary schools. A large and relatively stable Jewish community may account for the fact that both Friday and Saturday are half holidays, while Sunday is observed as a full holiday in the European pattern. Tunis and several secondary cities are important year-around tourist centers, giving Tunisia much wider contacts with people of non-Islamic culture than is the case in Libya. Yet the law against proselytism is rigidly enforced and very few native Tunisians belong to any of the churches in the country.

In *Algeria* at the peak of the French colonial period there were more than a million European residents, the majority of them Roman Catholics. When independence was achieved in 1963 about ninety percent of those foreigners left the country. Thus the number of Catholics was abruptly decimated, but they still comprise by far the largest Christian community in the country.

The French-born cardinal archbishop of Algiers, Léon-Etienne Duval, has maintained consistently good relationships with the Muslim majority in the country and with the government. When, under French colonial rule, the Catholics in Algeria enjoyed complete freedom of religious broadcasting by radio, it was Duval who demanded equal time for the Muslims. He openly championed Algerian independence, a highly unpopular cause among the French settlers in that day. And when independence came he, along with a number of French priests and religious sisters in the archdiocese, took Algerian citizenship.

Social and political transformation in Algeria since 1963 has been dramatic. Adult literacy has doubled, reaching a level of about 25 percent. But since more than two-thirds of the literate still read and write French only, the government has undertaken a vigorous program of Arabicization.

In 1980 the North Africa Mission (now called Arab World Ministries) reported the formation of "the first indigenous church among Muslims in North Africa." This tiny congregation is said to differ from other Protestant fellowship groups in the Maghrib in that it is composed entirely of baptized Christians, has a regular meeting place not provided by foreigners, and is responsible for its financial and administrative affairs.

In *Morocco* Islam is described by resident Europeans as "conservative but nondefensive"—more flexible than in Libya but more traditional than in either Tunisia or Algeria. The government is, however, concerned to secure the nation's Arabic and Islamic identity which they regard as threatened on two fronts: French and Spanish influences are too strongly perpetuated because most literate adults have learned to read and write in those languages rather than in Arabic. Moreover, the very large Berber population is non-Arab. The Berbers retain their tribal languages (although most of them also understand Arabic), and their practice of Islam is in some respects less than orthodox. Hence the Catholics in particular are prohibited from organizing churches or schools among the Berbers for political reasons. "The situation is very delicate because there may be more Berbers than Arabs in Morocco and the government is very cautious," said one priest.

In summary, the Christian penetration of North African society as a whole remains minimal. It is even less advanced today than in early centuries, and the rise of Arab nationalism has compounded the problem. It seems clear that Christian churches cannot expect to have wider influence without participating more heartily in the process of Arabicization now demanded by governments in all four countries. Unless and until that happens, Christians in Libya and the Maghrib will remain small, marginalized, and essentially foreign communities.

III. The Non-Arab Middle East: Turkey, Cyprus, and Iran

Turkey, Cyprus, and Iran are not part of the Arab world. That much they have in common, but in most other respects they could hardly be more dissimilar. Turkey, with its predominantly Sunni Muslim population, is a self-declared secular state. Yet Islamic social pressures remain so strong that the tiny Christian minority has gained little or no advantage from the formal disestablishment of Islam in 1928. Cyprus is the only country in the Middle East where Christians are a large majority of the population. For the first seventeen years of its modern existence as an autonomous state (1960-1977) the primate of the Orthodox Church of Cyprus was also head of state. Iran, with 98 percent of its population Muslim, is now a revolutionary Islamic Republic. The overthrow of a more religiously tolerant monarchy in 1979 has resulted in further restrictions and hardship to some, but not all, of the churches in that country.

The Republic of Turkey rose out of the ashes of the Ottoman Empire in 1923, under the vigorous leadership of Kemal Ataturk. Ataturk's purpose from the beginning was to create a secular state, free from the traditional and often reactionary Islamic complexion of Ottoman rule. Islam remained the de facto religion of the country, however, even after the clause that proclaimed it the religion of the state was stricken from the constitution in 1928. This is still the case. Christians in Turkey are no more than half of one percent of the country's population, and their number is declining. They belong almost entirely to non-Turkish ethnic minorities (Armenians, Greeks, Arabs, and others)[60] although the majority of them are Turkish citizens.

The nation continues to orient its political, legal, and economic structures along Western lines, but religiously it remains firmly a part of the Islamic world. Religious liberty is theoretically guaranteed in the new constitution of 1961, article 20, granting freedom of expression, individually and collectively, through spoken or written word. Mehmet Iskender notes that "while harassment of national [Christian] believers and eviction of foreign workers is not uncommon, there is no legal basis for such action, and Turkish courts of law since 1961 have invariably acquitted people tried for 'Christian propaganda.'"[61] In the popular mind, however, non-Islamic religious propaganda remains a crime, and the security forces look upon active proselytism as a disturbance of public order rather than an expression of religious freedom.

Whether or not the unremitting emigration of Christians from Turkey can be charged to "religious persecution" depends upon which interpretation one accepts. The Turkish government denies it categorically. The massacres of the 1920s, when the Syrian Orthodox with their own nationalistic ambitions shared the fate of the Armenians, are explained by the Turks as an unfortunate but necessary measure to secure the territorial integrity of the new nation. Many local Christians, on the other hand, insist that the brutality of the massacres more than sixty years ago, and the indignities still experienced by Christian minorities, reflect a religious intolerance that the official disestablishment of Islam has not alleviated.

In *Cyprus* the demographic picture is the reverse of that found elsewhere in the Middle East. It is the Muslims who insist that they have long been relegated to second-class citizenship by the large Christian majority.

In 1963 the Turkish-Cypriot community, then about eighteen

percent of the total population, broke its relationship with the government of the newly independent nation, alleging that President Makarios had tried to alter the constitution agreed on by Turkey, Greece, and Britain in 1959. According to their allegation, the Archbishop wanted to diminish their political rights and thereby strengthen his own authority.[62] The island was divided by a "Green Line," separating the two ethnic groups more or less effectively, although some intercommunication continued. A United Nations peacekeeping force arrived in 1964 and continues to this day.

No real progress was made toward reconciliation, however, and a much wider breach occurred in July 1974 when armed forces from mainland Turkey enabled the eighteen percent Turkish-Cypriot minority to occupy about forty percent of the island. In consequence as many as 180,000 Greek-Cypriots (one-third of the total) are said to have been made refugees in their own country. A considerable number of Turkish-Cypriots who had lived on the predominantly Greek side of the line were likewise dispossessed.

The Turkish-Cypriot sector, now covering most of the northern half of Cyprus, has substantially increased in population since 1974 by further immigration from mainland Turkey. With continuing moral and military support from the mainland, the Turkish-Cypriots declared themselves a fully autonomous state on November 15, 1983.

Two mutually exclusive nations now exist within the narrow confines of a small island, one of them composed entirely of Christians and the other entirely of Muslims. Thus Christian-Muslim relationships are no further along in the only segment of the Middle East that has a clear Christian majority than they are in the most conservative Muslim states. And here again the reasons for the impasse are political rather than religious.

Iran is the major stronghold of Shi'ite Islam in the world today. The population of the country is ninety-eight percent Muslim (ninety-three percent Shi'ite and five percent Sunni). The remaining two percent is equally divided between Christians and the other religious minorities (Jews, Zoroastrians, and Bahais).

Iran celebrated the 2500th anniversary of rule by monarchy in the summer of 1971. Only eight years later, in the spring of 1979, the Shah was deposed in a revolution of astounding rapidity, and an Islamic Republic proclaimed. The fact that the late Shah was quite hospitable to both Christians and Jews in the country does not increase their popularity with the new regime, certainly, but neither does it provoke hostility toward them on religious grounds as such. In Islamic jurisprudence Christians remain a "protected people," and the Muslim respect for Christ in accordance with Qu'ranic teaching is undiminished by the revolution. As recently as Christmas 1982 the Islamic Republic of Iran issued a twenty-rial postage stamp bearing the caption "Glorification of Christ's Birth."

The status of the traditional Eastern churches in Iran has been relatively unchanged by the 1979 revolution, but that is not the case with the Anglicans and Protestants. Their churches have historic relationships with missions from England and America, making them especially vulnerable in the current political climate. Moreover, the small membership of the Anglican and Protestant congregations include first-generation converts from Islam. The tiny Anglican Church has been stripped of its schools, hospitals, and other institutions and no longer has any legal recognition. Anglican bishop Hassan Deqani-Tafti, himself a convert from Islam, is in exile in England. Under the new regime, Muslim toleration of Christians clearly does not extend to those few who were born into the community of Islam but who chose Christian faith through baptism.

Islamic fundamentalism and a particularly strident nationalism now affect the Christians of Iran as deeply as those in any other Muslim country. Nevertheless the Christian minorities can ill afford to retreat into isolation from the proper social concerns of the new regime. They may now have an unprecedented opportunity to demonstrate that today's Christians continue to make their loyal contribution to their country's modern life.

Appendix A

ESTIMATED CHRISTIAN CONSTITUENCY
ACCORDING TO CHURCHES

	Constituency	*Percent of total Christian community*

I. *Eastern Orthodox Churches*

PATRIARCHATE OF ALEXANDRIA

Algeria	150	——
Egypt	7,000	0.13
Libya	700	2.00
Morocco	600	0.52
Sudan	1,800	0.20
Tunisia	200	3.32

PATRIARCHATE OF ANTIOCH

Iran	500	0.19
Iraq	520	0.15
Kuwait	6,000	14.60
Lebanon	300,000	22.30
Saudi Arabia	500	3.40
Syria	450,000	53.20
Turkey	2,000	1.57

PATRIARCHATE OF CONSTANTINOPLE

Turkey	8,000	6.30

PATRIARCHATE OF JERUSALEM

Israel (1947 borders)	30,000	31.50
Jordan	70,000	54.70
Palestine	37,000	53.74
(East Jerusalem, West Bank, Gaza)		

CHURCH OF CYPRUS

Cyprus	480,000	98.40

II. *Oriental Orthodox Churches*

ARMENIAN APOSTOLIC

Algeria	100	——
Cyprus	3,000	0.60
Egypt	12.000	0.23

Constituency	Percent of total Christian community
Iran 210,000	81.70
Iraq 14,000	4.07
Israel (1947 borders) 1,200	1.25
Jordan......................................3,000	2.34
Kuwait......................................6,600	16.03
Lebanon..............................200,000	14.85
Palestine.................................2,600	3.78
(East Jerusalem, West Bank, Gaza)	
Sudan...50	——
Syria...................................100,000	11.57
Turkey..................................60,000	47.20

COPTIC ORTHODOX

Algeria...................................1,500	1.83
Bahrain.....................................200	3.84
Egypt..................................5,000,000	95.03
Iraq..1,000	0.29
Israel (1947 borders)..................700	0.73
Jordan.....................................1,000	0.78
Kuwait.....................................1,300	3.16
Lebanon...................................2,000	0.15
Libya.....................................30,000	84.88
Palestine..................................2,500	3.63
(East Jerusalem, West Bank, Gaza)	
Saudi Arabia............................1,500	10.34
United Arab Emirates................600	5.97

SYRIAN ORTHODOX

Algeria......................................300	0.36
Bahrain......................................200	3.84
Egypt...400	——
Iraq..20,800	6.04
Israel (1947 borders)..................50	——
Jordan.....................................1,900	1.48
Kuwait.....................................2,100	5.10
Lebanon...................................15,000	1.11
Oman..125	7.55
Palestine............. 2,200	3.19
(East Jerusalem, West Bank, Gaza)	

	Constituency	*Percent of total* *Christian Community*
Saudi Arabia.	500	3.45
Syria	80,000	9.26
Turkey	35,000	27.55
United Arab Emirates	1,050	10.45

III. Assyrian ("Nestorian") Church of the East

Iran	15,000	5.80
Iraq	49,000	14.24
Kuwait	450	1.10
Lebanon	5,000	0.37
Palestine	800	1.16
(East Jerusalem, West Bank, Gaza)		
Syria	15,000	1.73

IV. Catholic Churches

ARMENIAN CATHOLIC

Cyprus	35	—
Egypt	1,000	—
Iran	2,000	0.78
Iraq	3,130	0.91
Israel (1947 borders)	50	—
Jordan	350	0.27
Kuwait	400	0.97
Lebanon	20,000	1.48
Palestine	250	—
(East Jerusalem, West Bank, Gaza)		
Syria	22,000	2.55
Turkey	4,500	3.54

CHALDEAN CATHOLIC

Egypt	750	—
Iran	15,000	5.83
Iraq	218,000	63.38
Kuwait	1,200	2.92
Lebanon	5,000	0.37
Syria	6,000	0.69
Turkey	6,000	4.72

Christian Constituency by Churches

Constituency	Percent of total Christian Community

COPTIC CATHOLIC

Constituency		Percent
Algeria	250	0.30
Egypt	100,000	1.90
Kuwait	200	0.48
Libya	1,200	3.39

GREEK (MELKITE) CATHOLIC

Constituency		Percent
Cyprus	200	—
Egypt	7,500	0.14
Iraq	400	—
Israel (1947 borders)	40,000	41.86
Jordan	19,000	14.83
Kuwait	3,000	7.29
Lebanon	260,000	19.31
Libya	350	0.99
Palestine	4,000	5.81
(East Jerusalem, West Bank, Gaza)		
Sudan	250	—
Syria	100,000	11.57

LATIN-RITE CATHOLIC

Constituency		Percent
Algeria	76,000	92.68
Bahrain	2,700	51.90
Cyprus	1,000	0.20
Egypt	6,000	0.11
Iran	7,000	2.72
Iraq	2,900	0.84
Israel (1947 borders)	12,000	12.56
Jordan	30,000	23.43
Kuwait	13,000	31.59
Lebanon	3,000	0.22
Libya	1,500	4.24
Morocco	110,000	96.07
Oman	700	42.30
Palestine	13,800	20.04
(East Jerusalem, West Bank, Gaza)		
Saudi Arabia.	5,000	34.48
Sudan	420,000	57.90
(Mostly in southern Black African provinces)		

	Constituency	*Percent of total Christian Community*
Syria.	10,000	1.16
Tunisia	5,000	82.98
Turkey	5,000	3.94
United Arab Emirates.	3,500	34.82

MARONITE CATHOLIC

Algeria.	150	—
Cyprus	3,000	0.61
Egypt.	4,000	—
Israel (1947 borders)	6,700	7.01
Kuwait.	1,900	4.61
Lebanon	500,000	37.14
Palestine.	250	0.36
(East Jerusalem, West Bank, Gaza)		
Sudan	50	—
Syria.	25,000	2.89

SYRIAN CATHOLIC

Algeria	100	0.12
Bahrain	200	3.84
Egypt	2,000	—
Iraq	31,000	9.01
Israel (1947 borders)	50	—
Kuwait	200	0.48
Lebanon	20,000	1.48
Palestine	450	0.65
(East Jerusalem, West Bank, Gaza)		
Syria	20,000	2.31
Turkey	1,500	1.18

V. Anglican Churches

Algeria	300	0.36
Bahrain	1,000	19.23
Cyprus	850	0.17
Egypt	1,000	—
Iran	2,600	1.01
Iraq	500	0.14
Israel (1947 borders)	1,100	1.15
Jordan	2,300	1.80
Kuwait	1,350	3.28

Christian Constituency by Churches

Constituency		Percent of total Christian Community
Lebanon	800	—
Libya	300	0.85
Morocco..	150	—
Oman	200	12.08
Palestine	2,400	3.48
(East Jerusalem, West Bank, Gaza)		
Saudi Arabia	1,000	6.89
Sudan	252,000	34.69
(Mostly in southern, Black African provinces)		
Tunisia	150	2.49
Turkey	300	0.24
United Arab Emirates	1,400	13.93

VI. Protestant Churches (Including Non-denominational, Independent Groups)

Algeria	2,550	3.10
Bahrain	1,100	21.15
Cyprus	285	—
Egypt	132,000	2.50
Iran	5,100	1.98
Iraq	2,720	0.79
Israel (1947 borders)	3,000	3.13
Jordan	1,500	1.17
Kuwait	3,350	8.14
Lebanon	19,800	1.47
Libya	1,290	3.65
Morocco	3,600	3.14
Oman	630	38.06
Palestine	2,000	2.90
(East Jerusalem, West Bank, Gaza)		
Saudi Arabia	5,000	34.48
Sudan	17,100	2.35
(Majority in southern, Black African provinces)		
Syria	18,000	2.08
Tunisia	575	9.54
Turkey	4,300	3.38
United Arab Emirates	2,500	24.87

ESTIMATED TOTAL CHRISTIAN CONSTITUENCY
ACCORDING TO COUNTRIES

Algeria

	% of total Christian community	% of total population
EASTERN ORTHODOX	0.6	——
Alexandria Patriarchate 150		
Russian 20		
Others 350		
ORIENTAL ORTHODOX	2.2	——
Coptic 1,500		
Syrian 300		
Armenian 100		
CATHOLIC	93.6	0.39
Latin-rite 76,000		
Coptic 250		
Maronite, Syrian 250		
PROTESTANT AND ANGLICAN	3.4	0.01
Eglise Protestante		
en Algérie 1,150		
Anglican 300		
Algerian Protestants		
of other mission		
origins 250		
Coptic Evangelical 250		
Other Arab and foreign		
Protestants 900		
TOTAL............82,000		0.43

Bahrain

ORIENTAL ORTHODOX	7.7
Syrian (Malabar)............ 200	
Coptic 200	

	% of total Christian community	% of total population
CATHOLIC 51.9		0.75

Total 2,700
      All under Latin-rite Capuchin
      priests; all services in English
      except when visiting clergy meet
      separately with Melkites, Maronites,
      Syrian, and Indian Catholics

PROTESTANT AND ANGLICAN 40.3   0.58
    Anglican. 1,000
    National Evangelical
      Church 450
    Mar Thomite 200
    Indian Brethren 100
    Church of South India 75
    Indian Pentecostal 75
    Awali Community 75
    St. Thomas Evangelical 25
    Other Protestants 100

TOTAL 5,200   1.43

Cyprus

EASTERN ORTHODOX.................................. 98.4   76.19
    Church of Cyprus 480,000

ORIENTAL ORTHODOX................................ 0.6   0.47
    Armenian Apostolic 3,000

CATHOLIC. 0.8   0.67
    Maronite 3,000
    Latin-rite......................... 1,000
      Mostly expatriates, military
      personnel not included
    Armenian 35
    Melkite 200

	% of total Christian community	% of total population

PROTESTANT AND ANGLICAN 0.2   0.17
    Anglicant 850
      All expatriates, military
      personnel not included
    Church of God of Prophecy 150
    Community Church, Nicosia 50
      Expatriates
    Greek Evangelical 35
    Christian Brethren 20
    Armenian Evangelical Union 15
    Seventh-day Adventist 15

TOTAL   488,000   77.50

Egypt

EASTERN ORTHODOX .... 0.1   ——
    Alexandria Patriarchate 7,000

ORIENTAL ORTHODOX.............................. 95.2   11.60
    Coptic 5,000,000
    Armenian........................ 12,000
    Syrian 400

CATHOLIC... 2.3   0.28
    Coptic 100,000
    Melkite 7,500
    Latin-rite 6,000
      Mostly expatriates
    Maronite 4,000
    Syrian 2,000
    Armenian.......................... 1,000
    Chaldean 750

PROTESTANT AND ANGLICAN 2.5   0.30
    Coptic Evangelical 100,000
      Synod of the Nile
    Anglican 1,000
      One-half expatriates

	% of total *Christian community*	*% of total* *population*

Other Protestants 32,000
    Assemblies of God, Christian
    Brethren, Free Methodist,
    Gospel Preaching Church,
    Pentecostal, Seventh-day
    Adventist, Church of God,
    Armenian Evangelical, Churches
    of Christ

TOTAl. 5,261,000   12.18

*Iran**

EASTERN ORTHODOX .... 0.3   —
    Greek 500
        Administratively related
        to Antioch Patriarchate
    Russian 400

ORIENTAL ORTHODOX 81.7   0.50
    Armenian Apostolic 210,000

ASSYRIAN ("NESTORIAN") 5.8   0.04
    Assyrian Church of
        the East 15,000

CATHOLIC... 9.0   0.06
    Chaldean 15,000
    Latin-rite 7,000
        Mostly expatriates
    Armenian 2,000

PROTESTANT AND ANGLICAN..................... 3.1   0.02
    Evangelical Church
        of Iran 3,000
    Anglican (Episcopal
        Diocese) 2,600
        One-half expatriates
    Assemblies of God 665

	% of total Christian community	% of total population
Other Protestants .... 1,435 One-half expatriates		
TOTAL 256,850		0.62

* Estimates as of 1979

Iraq

	% of total Christian community	% of total population
EASTERN ORTHODOX .... 0.1 Antioch Patriarchate 520	0.1	—
ORIENTAL ORTHODOX .... 10.4 Syrian .... 20,800 Armenian .... 14,000 Coptic 1,000	10.4	0.26
ASSYRIAN ("NESTORIAN") .... 14.2 Assyrian Church of the East 49,000	14.2	0.35
CATHOLIC ....74.3 Chaldean .... 218,000 Syrian .... 31,000 Armenian .... 3,130 Latin-rite .... 2,900 Melkite 400	74.3	1.85
PROTESTANT AND ANGLICAN .... 0.9 Evangelical Church .... 1,275 Anglican .... 500 Mostly expatriates Seventh-day Adventists.... 175 All other Protestants 1,270	0.9	0.02
TOTAL 343,970		2.48

	% of total Christian community	*% of total population*

*Israel**

EASTERN ORTHODOX 31.5		0.86
Jerusalem Patriarchate .. 30,000		
Russian.............................. 150		
ORIENTAL ORTHODOX 2.6		0.07
Armenian 1,200		
Coptic 700		
Syrian 50		
Ethiopian........................... 50		
CATHOLIC 61.5		1.68
Melkite 40,000		
Latin-rite 12,000		
Maronite 6,700		
Syrian 50		
Armenian 50		
PROTESTANT AND ANGLICAN 4.3		0.12
Episcopal Church		
(Anglican) 1,100		
Protestant 3,000		
Baptist, Brethren, Churches of		
Christ, Church of God of Prophecy,		
Christian and Missionary Alliance,		
Church of Scotland Mission, Lutheran		
(Norwegian and Scandinavian Seamen),		
Seventh-day Adventist, Nazarene,		
various independent groups		
TOTAL 95,550		2.73

* 1947 borders

	% of total *Christian community*	*% of total* *population*

Jordan

EASTERN ORTHODOX 54.7   3.06
    Jerusalem Patriarchate ...70,000

ORIENTAL ORTHODOX 3.8   0.26
    Armenian 3,000
    Syrian 1,900
    Coptic 1,000

CATHOLIC 38.5   2.16
    Latin-rite 30,000
    Melkite 19,000
    Armenian 350

PROTESTANT AND ANGLICAN 2.9   0.17
    Episcopal (Anglican) 2,300
    Protestant 1,500
        Free Evangelical, Baptist,
        Christian and Missionary
        Alliance, Nazarene, Assemblies
        of God, Bible Preaching Church,
        Seventh-day Adventist

TOTAL 128,050   5.65

Kuwait

EASTERN ORTHODOX 14.6   0.40
    Antioch Patriarch............. 6,000

ORIENTAL ORTHODOX 24.3   0.66
    Armenian Apostolic........ 6,600
    Syrian (Malabar) 2,100
    Coptic 1,300

ASSYRIAN ("NESTORIAN") .... 1.1   ——
    Assyrian Church of the
        East 450

	% of total Christian community	% of total population
CATHOLIC	48.6	1.33
Latin-rite 13,000		
Melkite 3,000		
Maronite 1,900		
Chaldean 1,200		
Armenian 400		
Syrian 200		
Coptic 200		
PROTESTANT AND ANGLICAN	11.4	0.31
Anglican 1,350		
Protestant 3,350		
Mar Thoma, National		
Evangelical Church,		
Church of South India,		
Christian Brethren,		
Indian Brethren, Seventh-		
day Adventist		
TOTAL 41,150		2.70

Lebanon

	% of total Christian community	% of total population
EASTERN ORTHODOX	22.3	10.00
Antioch Patriarchate.... 300,000		
Russian (Moscow		
Patriarchate) 200		
Russian (non-Moscow) 100		
ORIENTAL ORTHODOX	16.1	7.23
Armenian Apostolic 200,000		
Syrian 15,000		
Coptic 2,000		
ASSYRIAN ("NESTORIAN") 0.4		0.16
Assyrian Church of		
the East 5,000		
CATHOLIC	59.6	26.76
Maronite 500,000		
Melkite 260,000		

Appendix B

		% of total Christian community	% of total population

Armenian 20,000
Syrian........................... 20,000
Chaldean 5,000
Latin-rite ...,..................... 3,000

PROTESTANT AND ANGLICAN 1.5   0.68
    National Evangelical
        Synod 10,000
    Armenian Evangelical
        Union 5,000
    Anglican and Arab
        Episcopal 800
    Other Protestants 4,800
        Baptist (various groups),
        National Evangelical Church,
        Church of God, Assemblies of
        God, Seventh-day Adventists,
        Church of the Nazarene, Churches
        of Christ, independent missions

TOTAL   1,345,950   44.83

Libya

EASTERN ORTHODOX......................................2.0   ——
    Alexandria Patriarchate 700

ORIENTAL ORTHODOX 84.9   0.11
    Coptic 30,000
        All expatriates

CATHOLIC (all expatriates) ....8.6   ——
    Latin-rite 1,500
    Coptic 1,200
    Melkite 350

PROTESTANT AND ANGLICAN.......................4.5   ——
    All expatriates
    Anglican 300
    Protestant 1,290
        Union Church (Tripoli),
        Baptist, Churches of Christ,

	% of total *Christian community*	*% of total* *population*

Coptic Evangelical, Seventh-
day Adventist

TOTAL.........................35,340   0.14

Morocco

EASTERN ORTHODOX .... 0.7   —
    Alexandria Patriarchate 600
    Russian 160
      One congregation Moscow-
      related, one White Russian

CATHOLIC.. 96.0   0.52
    Latin-rite 110,000
      Almost all expatriates

PROTESTANT AND ANGLICAN .... 3.3   —
    Anglican............................. 150
      All expatriates
    Moroccan Protestants........... 200
    Foreign Protestants 3,400
      French Reformed, Assemblies
      of God, Holiness, Christian
      Brethren, Churches of Christ,
      Seventh-day Adventist

TOTAL.........................114,500   0.54

Oman

ORIENTAL ORTHODOX 7.5   0.01
    Syrian (Malabar) 125

CATHOLIC.. 42.3   0.08
    Latin-rite 700
      All expatriates

PROTESTANT AND ANGLICAN 50.1   0.09
    Total 830
      Protestant Church of Oman

	% of total Christian community	% of total population

(Protestant and Anglican)
mainly expatriates but
including some native Omanis,
Mar Thomite, Indian Pentecostal,
Indian Brethren

TOTAL...1,655   0.18

Palestine
(East Jerusalem, West Bank, Gaza)

EASTERN ORTHODOX 54.5   2.27
    Jerusalem Patriarchate   37,000
    Russian 300
    Romanian 250

ORIENTAL ORTHODOX 10.7   0.44
    Armenian 2,600
    Coptic. 2,500
    Syrian 2,200
    Ethiopian 50

CATHOLIC 27.2   1.14
    Latin-rite 13,800
    Melkite 4,000
    Syrian 450
    Armenian 250
    Maronite 250

ASSYRIAN ("NESTORIAN").............................1.2   ——
    Assyrian Church of
        the East 800

PROTESTANT AND ANGLICAN 6.4   0.26
    Episcopal Church
        (Anglican) 2,400
    Protestant 2,000
        Evangelical Lutheran,
        Baptist, Church of the
        Nazarene, Church of God
        of Prophecy, Assemblies of God,

	% of total Christian community	% of total population

Bible Presbyterian,
various independent groups

TOTAL.............................68,850   4.11

Saudi Arabia
(Christians all expatriates)

EASTERN ORTHODOX .... 3.4   ——
    Antioch Patriarchate 500
    No organized congregations

ORIENTAL ORTHODOX .... 13.8   ——
    Coptic and Syrian 2,000
    No organized congregations

CATHOLIC.. 41.4   ——
    All rites 6,000

PROTESTANT AND ANGLICAN.....................41.4   ——
    Anglican...................... 1,000
        Diocese of Cyprus and
        the Gulf
    Protestant 5,000
        ARAMCO community churches
        (American and European),
        Mar Thomite, Church of South
        India, Indian Brethren, Churches
        of Christ, house churches

TOTAL.............................14,500   0.14

Sudan

	Northern (Arabic speaking)	Southern (Black African)

EASTERN ORTHODOX
    Alexandria Patriarchate 1,800   ——

Appendix B

	Northern (Arabic speaking)	Southern (Black African)

ORIENTAL ORTHODOX

Coptic	30,000	——
Ethiopian	5,000	——
Armenian	50	——

CATHOLIC

Latin-rite	20,000	400,000
Melkite	250	——
Maronite	50	——

PROTESTANT AND ANGLICAN
Episcopal (Anglican)

Diocese of Sudan.	2,000	250,000
Protestant (total)	12,800	4,300

Presbyterian Church of Sudan,
Church of East Central Sudan,
Sudanese Church of Christ,
Evangelical Church of Sudan,
Evangelical Revival Church,
Seventh-day Adventist, Baptist,
independent congregations

TOTAL	71,950	654,300

Percentages in the Country as a Whole

	% of total Christian community	% of total population
EASTERN ORTHODOX	0.2	——
ORIENTAL ORTHODOX	4.8	0.18
CATHOLIC	57.9	2.14
PROTESTANT AND ANGLICAN	37.1	1.37
		3.69

	% of total Christian community	% of total population

Syria

EASTERN ORTHODOX 53.2 4.94
Antioch Patriarchate .. 450,000

ORIENTAL ORTHODOX 21.3 1.98
Armenian..................... 100,000
Syrian 80,000

ASSYRIAN ("NESTORIAN") 1.7 0.16
Assyrian Church of
the East 15,000

CATHOLIC 21.6 2.01
Melkite 100,000
Maronite 25,000
Armenian........................22,000
Syrian 20,000
Latin-rite 10,000
Chaldean 6,000

PROTESTANT 2.1 0.20
Total 18,000
Armenian Evangelical Union,
National Evangelical Synod,
Christian and Missionary
Alliance, Church of God
(Anderson, IN), Church of God
(Cleveland, TN), Evangelical
Church in Damascus, Nazarene,
Armenian Brethren, Seventh-day
Adventist, Assemblies of God,
independent congregations

TOTAL 864,000 9.29

Tunisia

EASTERN ORTHODOX ....5.0 —
Alexandria Patriarchate...... 200
Russian (non-Moscow
related) 25
Others 75

	% of total Christian community	% of total population
CATHOLIC 83.0		—
Latin-rite 5,000		
PROTESTANT AND ANGLICAN 12.0		—
Anglican 150		
French Reformed 150		
Other Protestants................ 425		
Pentecostal, Evangelical house groups, Christian Brethren, Seventh-day Adventist, North Africa Mission		
TOTAL 6,025*		—

* All but a handful in any of the communions represented are expatriates or people of foreign extraction.

Turkey

	% of total Christian community	% of total population
EASTERN ORTHODOX 9.6		—
Constantinople Patriarchate 8,000		
Antioch Patriarchate 2,000		
In Antakya and Alexandretta		
Others (Russian, Serbian) 2,200		
ORIENTAL ORTHODOX 74.8		0.20
Armenian 60,000		
Syrian 35,000		
CATHOLIC.. 12.2		—
Chaldean 6,000		
Latin-rite 5,000		
Armenian 4,500		
Syrian 1,500		

	% of total Christian community	% of total population
PROTESTANT AND ANGLICAN 3.4		——

Anglican 300
   Mainly expatriates
Expatriate Protestants 1,500
   Excluding military
All other Protestants 2,800
   Armenian Evangelical,
   Worldwide Missions,
   Pentecostal, Christian
   Brethren, Greek Evangelical,
   Seventh-day Adventist,
   Operation Mobilization,
   various independent groups

TOTAL 127,000   0.28

United Arab Emirates

Abu Dhabi, Ajman, al-Fujeirah, Dubai, Ras al Khaimah, Sharjah, Umm al-Quwein

ORIENTAL ORTHODOX 16.4   0.17
   Syrian (Malabar) 750
   Coptic, Syrian (Antioch).... 900

CATHOLIC 44.7   0.46
   All rites 4,500

PROTESTANT AND ANGLICAN 38.8   0.39
   Anglican/Community
     churches 1,400
   Protestant (total) 2,500
     Mar Thomite, Evangelical
     Alliance Mission, Indian
     Pentecostal, Indian Brethren,
     Arab Evangelical

TOTAL 10,050   1.02

NOTES

1. The definition adopted by the majority at the Council of Chalcedon, and thereafter the official position of Eastern Orthodox, Roman Catholic (and by extension, Protestant) churches, is that Christ has two clearly distinguishable natures, human and divine. Each nature is perfect in itself and distinct from the other, yet perfectly united in the one Person who is at once God and man. The fear of the "non-Chalcedonians" is that this definition leans in the direction of compromising Christ's deity which they emphasize above all else.

2. The Archbishop of Cyprus is the only head of a church to be elected by universal suffrage rather than by an ecclesiastical or politically representative body. See *1978 Yearbook of the Orthodox Church*, p. 160.

3. In Nicolae Mihaita, ed., *Orthodox Youth and the Ecumenical Movement*, p. 66.

4. Markides Kyriacos, *The Rise and Fall of the Cyprus Republic*, p. 55.

5. *Eastern Churches News Letter*, new series, no. 15, autumn 1982, p. 25.

6. Thomas is said to have spent seven years in ministry near Lake Urmia (in the north of modern Iran) en route to India. Eusebius (ca. 260-340), "the father of church history," supports this tradition in his *Ecclesiastical History*, III, 1, where he credits St. Thomas with evangelizing the Parthians.

7. Centuries ago when communication with the center of the Church of the East became virtually impossible the vast majority (now more than two million) of the South Indian "Nestorians" came under the jurisdiction of the Syrian Orthodox Patriarchate of Antioch.

8. The late Mar Ishai Shimun XXI married at the end of his long tenure in the patriarchal office, claiming the precedent of early centuries, but it was unacceptable to his people.

9. Two additional dioceses in Iraq are loyal solely to the dissident patriarch, encouraged by the Iraqi government because he is an Iraqi citizen.

10. Aubrey R. Vine, *The Nestorian Churches*, p. 208.

11. Neither the Armenian Church nor the Ethiopian people were actually present at the Council of Chalcedon. The Ethiopians at that time (and for the next sixteen centuries until 1958) were subject to the Coptic Patriarch of Alexandria. The Armenian Church was prevented from attendance because of events in Armenia, but within the next sixty years had aligned itself solidly with the non-Chalcedonian party. See Karekin Sarkissian, *The Council of Chalcedon and the Armenian Church*, passim.

12. The Armenians follow an ancient custom, historically reversed by some of the other churches, in regarding the office of a catholicos as higher than that of a patriarch. In the Armenian use of those terms, a catholicos governs the church in several countries, whereas a patriarch rules in only one. Thus the Patriarchs of Jerusalem and Constantinople—both ultimately responsible to the Echmiadzin Catholicosate—exercise authority only in Jerusalem-Jordan and Turkey respectively.

13. See the chapter by K. V. Sarkissian (now Catholicos Karekin II) in A. J. Arberry, ed., *Religion in the Middle East,* volume 1, pp. 516-517.

14. A more detailed description is given by Jean Corbon, "Le Catholicossat Arménien de la Grande Maison de Cilicie," p. 7.

15. Ibid., pp. 17-20.

16. See Otto F. A. Meinardus, "The Coptic Church in Egypt," in A. J. Arberry, op. cit., for an elaboration of this and a concise summary of Coptic Church history up to the early 1960s.

17. Four monasteries are in Wadi'l-Natrun: St. Macarius, St. Bishay, Deir al-Suryan, and Deir al-Baramus; St. Anthony and St. Paul the Theban are in the eastern desert; Deir al-Muharraq and St. Samuel are north of Assiut; St. Minas (the newest, founded in 1959) is at Maryut.

18. Fr. Jean Corbon, a Catholic theologian in Beirut has suggested using the term "Ephesian Churches" for this group of Armenian, Coptic, and Syrian communities, since they all regard the Council of Ephesus (A.D. 431) as the last authoritative ecumenical council. See his "Le Catholicossat Arménien de la Grande Maison de Cilicie," p. 10.

19. Mar Ignatius Zakka I Iwas, *The Syrian Orthodox Church of Antioch at a Glance,* pp. 4, 20-21.

20. See Norman A. Horner, "Tur Abdin: A Christian Minority Struggles to Preserve Its Identity."

21. For details of the early Roman Catholic-Eastern Churches encounter see G. C. Anawati, "The Roman Catholic Church and Churches in Communion with Rome," in A. J. Arberry, ed., op. cit., pp. 347-417. Anawati refers to this incident on p. 380.

22. G. C. Anawati, ibid, pp. 366-367, is the source of information condensed in this brief paragraph.

23. The addition of "Alexandria and Jerusalem" to this title was made by Rome only in 1856. Prior to that date it had been merely "Antioch and All the East."

24. Robert B. Betts, *Christians in the Arab East,* p. 143.

25. Beginning with Patriarch Maximos IV Saigh (1947-1967). See ibid., p. 151.

26. Information in this and the following two paragraphs is based on concise resumes of early Armenian Catholic history in Edouard Serabian, ed., *Bzoummar à Travers l'Histoire,* and in G. C. Anawati, op. cit.

27. The most widely known Armenian Catholic Patriarch in recent decades was Cardinal Gregory Peter Agaganian, who resigned the patriarchal office to accept duties in Rome and was twice a possible candidate for the papacy.

28. Historical details in this and the preceding paragraph are cited and elaborated in Donald Attwater, *The Uniate Churches of the East* and in Joseph Hajjar, *Les*

Chrétiens Uniates du Proche Orient, and in Raymond Etteldorf, *The Catholic Church in the Middle East.*

29. The foregoing paragraph is a brief summary of information given by G. C. Anawati, op. cit., pp. 369-370.

30. In 1965 four of the six patriarchs of the Eastern-rite churches held the rank of Cardinal: Syrian, Melkite, Maronite, and Coptic. The Syrian, Melkite, and Maronite patriarchs of that date are now deceased, and only the Maronite patriarch's successor was named (in 1983) to replace him in the Cardinalate.

31. See *Annuaire de l'Eglise Catholique en Terre Sainte,* 1979, p. 10. Two other Latin Patriarchates were abandoned after relatively brief periods and never reinstated: Antioch (1098-1267) and Constantinople (1204-1261).

32. A booklet, *The Christians of Kuwait,* was published locally by Msgr. Victor Sanmiguel, Apostolic Vicar for Kuwait in 1970. A more recent effort to describe the Christian churches in the Arabian Gulf area as a whole, is Norman A. Horner, "Present-day Christianity in the Gulf States of the Arabian Peninsula," 1978.

33. *Annuaire de l'Eglise Catholique en Terre Sainte,* 1979.

34. The Latin Patriarchal Seminary (Jerusalem), the International Franciscan Seminary (Jerusalem), the Salesian Seminary (Bethlehem), and the Passionist Seminary (Jerusalem).

35. Fifteen related directly to the patriarchate, eighteen maintained by male religious orders, and twenty-seven by female religious orders.

36. As of 1970, before the outbreak of extensive warfare in Lebanon, the Catholic religious institutes (both Latin- and Eastern-rite) directed a total of 282 schools, two universities, thirteen hospitals, twenty-three orphanages, and three old-people's homes. See *Al Montada,* No. 40/41, Nov. 1970 to Jan. 1971, pp. 31ff.

37. See Mohamed Omer Beshir, *The Southern Sudan: Background to Conflict,* p. 82.

38. This token collaboration is reminiscent of an early and much larger joint enterprise of Anglicans with Lutherans. The first Anglican Bishop in Jerusalem, Michael Solomon Alexander (1841-45) was named jointly by the crowns of Prussia and England, in a mission initiated and largely funded by King Frederick William IV of Prussia.

39. For a vivid and personalized account of this church's experience in the new Islamic Republic, see H. B. Dehqani-Tafti, *The Hard Awakening.*

40. Up-to-date summaries of Anglican activities in Egypt are given in *Bridgehead,* a mimeographed periodical distributed by All Saints Cathedral in Cairo.

41. There are virtually no native Libyan Christians of any denomination living in the country. The few Libyan converts made through missionary efforts, chiefly by independent Protestant groups, have emigrated for reasons of security and employment to southern France and elsewhere.

42. Anglican work in Morocco is under the Diocese of Gibraltar.

43. This total does not include people on the two large British military bases in Cyprus. Their religious activities are for the most part quite separate from those of the established parishes and less related to the overall Christian impact in the country.

44. Anglican priest Peter Cowen opened the former Orthodox monastery to ecumenical study groups in 1972, and was the first chairman of the interchurch governing board after the monastery's renovation to become the Aiya Napa Conference Center in 1976.

45. This church became an autonomous Province in 1976, after the restructuring of the Jerusalem Archdiocese to which it formerly belonged.

46. Most of the Protestant churches here listed are known personally by this writer and were more briefly described in my *Rediscovering Christianity Where It Began*. Those churches were revisited in 1983 and the membership statistics revised accordingly. For groups I do not personally know but which have been incorporated in the present volume, I have depended on figures given by David B. Barrett in his *World Christian Encyclopedia* (1982).

47. See statistical tables in Julius Richter, *A History of Protestant Missions in the Near East*, p. 419.

48. Estimate of Melkite Archbishop Lufti Laham in conversation with Paul A. Hopkins in October 1982, cited in Hopkins' unpublished report of his visit on behalf of the United Presbyterian Church, U.S.A. I also learned from Armenian Orthodox sources that the Armenian community alone in and around Jerusalem has decreased from 15,000 in 1947 to less than 3,000 at present.

49. Ray G. Register, Jr., "Christian Witness in the State of Israel Today," p. 16.

50. See Robert B. Betts, op. cit., pp. 170-172 for names and positions of specific Christians prominent in Jordan's political life from 1948 to 1970.

51. A contemptuous statement attributed to Israel's former prime minister, Menachem Begin, and widely used by Israel to justify its refusal to consider establishment of an autonomous Palestinian state in the West Bank and Gaza: "The Palestinians already have a country; it is called Jordan."

52. No official census has been taken since 1932. An unofficial estimate was published on November 5, 1975 in *An-Nahar*, Beirut's prestigious newspaper, owned and operated by Greek Orthodox Christians. This estimate gave a combined Muslim and Druze total of about 2,000,000 and a Christian total of roughly 1,200,000. The numbers are obviously different thirteen years later, in 1988, but the ratio is probably not much changed.

53. These percentages are from an unpublished but meticulous study by a French Dominican missionary of forty years service in Iraq.

54. There are still some totally Christian villages in northern Iraq, the most prominent of them being Karakesh (Syrian Catholic), Karamlès (Chaldean Catholic), and Bartolla (Syrian Orthodox).

55. The World Council of Churches maintained a refugee service in Beirut for a

121

number of years. Through the 1970s that office arranged passage and relocation of Iraqi Christians, among others, who alleged "religious persecution" as the reason for emigration.

56.   In 1971 the Iraqi representative of the United Bible Societies in Baghdad was summarily imprisoned after his office had been ransacked by the police. He was later released, without explanation, through intervention from outside Iraq.

57.   The largest Christian communities are Indian. Although India itself is hardly more than two percent Christian, Indian Christians have been more inclined than Hindus to work abroad. Thus as many as 30 percent of the Indians in the Arabian Gulf States may be Christians.

58.   Joseph J. Malone, *The Arab Lands of Western Asia*, p. 232.

59.   For a more detailed description of the various churches and their situation, see Norman A. Horner, "Christianity in North Africa Today."

60.   The Orthodox churches have no ethnic Turks in their membership, and Catholic and Protestant churches have very few. Local Catholics say "perhaps 200." Protestants claim a slightly larger number, but Mehmet Iskender, an evangelical leader in Turkey, disputes that claim. *In The Gospel and Islam: A 1978 Compendium*, ed. by Don McCurry, p. 283, Iskender writes: "In the whole country the number of converted Muslims attending with any regularity a fellowship or church would number about 20—about one for every two million of the population."

61.   Mehmet Iskender, "The Comparative Status of Christianity and Islam in Turkey," in Don McCurry, op. cit., p. 282.

62.   Roderick H. Davidson, *Turkey*, p. 159.

SELECTED BIBLIOGRAPHY

BOOKS

Albino, Oliver. *The Sudan: A Southern Viewpoint*. London: Oxford University Press, 1970.

Annuaire de l'Eglise Catholique en Terre Sainte. Jerusalem: Latin Patriarchate, 1979.

Arberry, A. J., ed. *Religion in the Middle East* (2 volumes). Cambridge: Cambridge University Press, 1969.

Armajani, Yahya. *Iran* (The Modern Nations in Historical Perspective series). Englewood Cliffs, New Jersey: Prentice-Hall, Inc., 1972.

Atiya, Aziz. *A History of Eastern Christianity*. London, Methuen & Co., 1967 and Notre Dame, Ind.: Notre Dame University Press, 1968.

Attalides, Michael. *Cyprus: Nationalism and International Politics*. Edinburgh: Q Press, 1979.

Attwater, Donald. *The Uniate Churches of the East*. London: Geoffrey Chapman, 1961.

Baker, Derek, ed. *The Orthodox Churches and the West* (volume 13 of Studies in Church History). Oxford: Basil Blackwell, 1976.

Barrett, David B., ed. *World Christian Encyclopedia: A Comparative Survey of Churches and Religions in the Modern World, A.D. 1900-2000*. Nairobi: Oxford University Press, 1982.

Beshir, Mohammed Omer. *The Southern Sudan: Background to Conflict*. Khartoum: Khartoum University Press, 1970.

Betts, Robert B. *Christians in the Arab East*. Atlanta: John Knox Press, 1978.

Bria, Ion, ed. *Martyria/Mission: The Witness of the Orthodox Churches Today*. Geneva: World Council of Churches, Commission on World Mission and Evangelism, 1980.

Colbi, Saul P. *Christianity in the Holy Land Past and Present*. Tel Aviv: Am Hassefer Publishers, Ltd., 1969.

Constantelos, Demetrios J., ed. *Orthodox Theology and Diaku*
Brookline, Massachusetts: Hellenic College Press, 198
especially chapters by Vasil Istavrides on the Antioch ᴀnu
Constantinople Patriarchates.

Davison, Roderic H. *Turkey* (The Modern Nations in Historical
Perspective series). Englewood Cliffs, New Jersey: Prentice-Hall,
Inc., 1968.

Dehqani-Tafti, Hassan. *Design of My World*. New York: Association
Press, 1959.

──────. *The Hard Awakening*. New York: The Seabury Press,
1981.

Dib, Pierre. *Histoire de l'Eglise Maronite* (2 volumes). Beirut:
Archevêché Maronite, 1962.

Etteldorf, Raymond. *The Catholic Church in the Middle East*. New
York: Macmillan, 1959.

Grabill, Joseph J. *Protestant Diplomacy and the Near East: Missionary
Influence on American Policy, 1810-1927*. Minneapolis: University
of Minnesota Press, 1971.

Hackett, John. *A History of the Orthodox Church of Cyprus*. London:
Methuen & Co., 1901. Reprinted 1972, New York: Burt Franklin.

Hajjar, Joseph. *Les Chrétiens Uniates du Proche Orient*. Paris:
Editions du Seuil, 1962.

Hintlian, Kevork. *History of the Armenians in the Holy Land*.
Jerusalem: St. James Press, 1976.

Horner, Norman A. *Rediscovering Christianity Where It Began: A
Survey of Contemporary Churches in the Middle East and Ethiopia*.
Beirut: Near East Council of Churches, 1974.

Hourani, Albert H. *Minorities in the Arab World*. London: Oxford
University Press, 1947.

Iwas, Mar Ignatius Zakka I. *The Syrian Orthodox Church of Antioch at a
Glance*. Aleppo, Syria: privately printed by Metropolitan Grego-
rios Youhanna Ibrahim, 1981. (In English and Arabic. The
English section is pp 1-25.)

Janin, R. P. *The Separated Eastern Churches* (tr. from French).
London: Sands & Co., 1933.

Jessup, Henry H. *Fifty-three Years in Syria* (2 volumes). New York: Revell & Co., 1910.

Joseph, John. *The Nestorians and Their Muslim Neighbors*. Princeton, New Jersey: Princeton University Press, 1961.

Jurji, Edward J. *The Middle East: Its Religion and Culture*. Philadelphia: Westminster Press, 1956.

Kawerau, Peter. *Die Jakobitische Kirche im Zeitalter der Syrichen Renaissance*. Berlin: Walter de Gruyter, 1960.

Keshishian, Aram. *The Witness of the Armenian Church in a Diaspora Situation*. New York: Prelacy of the Armenian Apostolic Church of America, 1978.

Keshishian, Kevork K. *Nicosia, Capital of Cyprus: Then and Now*. Nicosia: Moufflon Book Center, 1978.

Kidd, B. T. *The Churches of Eastern Christendon*. London: The Faith Press, 1927.

Kwarme, Ole Chr., ed. *Let Jews and Arabs Hear His Voice*. Jerusalem: The United Christian Council in Israel, 1981.

Leroy, Jules. *Monks and Monasteries of the Near East*. London: Harrap, 1963.

Malone, Joseph J. *The Arab Lands of Western Asia*. Englewood Cliffs, New Jersey: Prentice-Hall, Inc., 1973.

Markides, Kyriacos C. *The Rise and Fall of the Cyprus Republic*. New Haven, Connecticut and London: Yale University Press, 1977.

Mayes, Stanley. *Makarios: Life and Leadership*. London: Abelard-Schuman, 1979.

McCurry, Don, ed. *The Gospel and Islam: A 1978 Compendium*. Monrovia, California: Missions Advanced Research and Communication Center, 1979.

Meinardus, Otto F. A. *Christian Egypt: Faith and Life*. Cairo: American University in Cairo Press, 1970.

Mihaita, Nicolas, ed. *Orthodox Youth and the Ecumenical Movement*. Geneva: World Student Christian Federation, 1978.

Parry, O. H. *Six Months in a Syrian Monastery*. London: H. Cox, 1895.

Peroncel-Hugoz, Jean-Pierre. *Le Radeau de Mahomet*. Paris: Lieu Commun, 9, rue Bernard-Palissy, Paris VI, 1983. (See especially pp. 117-144 concerning the Coptic enigma and Pope Shenooda's banishment.)

Proc, Alex, ed. *Yearbook of the Orthodox Church*. Munich: Verlag Alex Proc, 1978. (This work is published annually, but not in the same language each year.)

Richter, Julius. *A History of Protestant Mission in the Near East*. New York: Fleming H. Revell Co., 1910.

Rondot, Pierre. *Les Chrétiens d'Orient*. Paris: J. Peyronnet & Cie., 1955.

Salama, Adib Najib. *A History of the Evangelical Church in Egypt, 1854- 1980*. Cairo: Dar al-Thaqafa, 1982. (In Arabic.)

Salibi, Kamal. *Crossroads to Civil War—Lebanon 1958-76*. Delmar, New York: Caravan Books, 1976.

Sarkissian, Kerakin. *The Council of Chalcedon and the Armenian Church*. New York: Prelacy of the Armenian Apostolic Church of America, 1965.

————. *The Witness of the Oriental Orthodox Churches*. Beirut: privately printed, 1968.

Sayegh, M. [Patriarch Maximos IV] *Catholicisme ou Latinisme*. Harissa, Lebanon: Melkite Patriarchal Press, 1962.

Serabian, Edouard, ed. *Bzoummar à Travers l'Histoire*. Beirut: Armenian Catholic Patriarchate, 1979. (Published in celebration of the 300th anniversary of the birth of Abraham-Pierre I Ardzivian, first Armenian Catholic Patriarch.)

Vander Werff, Lyle L. *Christian Mission to Muslims: Anglican and Reformed Approaches in India and the Near East, 1800-1938*. South Pasadena, California: William Carey Library, 1977.

Vanezis, P. N. Makarios: *Life and Leadership*. London: Abelard-Schuman, 1979.

von Dessein, Eberhard and Paul Löffler, eds. *Christen im Mittleren Osten*. Frankfurt am Main: Evangelische Mittelost-Kommission, 1981.

Vine, Aubrey R. *The Nestorian Churches*. London: The Independent Press, 1937.

Wakim, Edward. *The Lonely Minority*. New York: Morrow, 1963.

Waterfield, Robin E. *Christians in Persia*. London: George Allen & Unwin, 1973.

Wigram, W. A. *The Assyrians and Their Neighbors*. London: G. Bell and Sons, 1929.

ARTICLES IN PERIODICALS

Badeau, John S. "The Role of the Missionary in the Near East." *International Review of Missions*, October 1954, pp. 397-403.

Bridgehead, a monthly mimeographed publication, Cairo: All Saints Cathedral, gives up-to-date information about Anglican churches throughout the Middle East.

Corbon, Jean. "Le Catholicossat Arménien de la Grande Maison de Cilicie." *Courrier Oecumenique*, No. 12, 1981 (Beirut: Commission for Ecumenical Relations of the Catholic Patriarchs and Bishops of Lebanon), pp. 5ff.

Horner, Norman A. "Ancient Churches—Alive and Well." *New World Outlook*, November 1977, pp. 31-33.

———. "Christianity in North Africa Today." *Occasional Bulletin of Missionary Research*, April 1980, pp. 83-88.

———. "The Churches and the Crisis in Lebanon." *Occasional Bulletin of Missionary Research*, January 1977, pp 8-12.

———. "An East African Orthodox Church." *Journal of Ecumenical Studies*, Spring 1975, pp. 221-233.

———. "Ecumenical Roadblocks in the Middle East." *Worldmission*, Summer 1978, pp. 11-17.

———. "Is Christianity at Home in Iran?" *Occasional Bulletin of Missionary Research*, October 1979, pp 151-155.

———. "The Problem of Intra-Christian Proselytism." *International Review of Mission*, October 1981, pp. 304-313.

———. "Tur Abdin: A Christian Minority Struggles to Preserve Its Identity." *Occasional Bulletin of Missionary Research*, October 1978, pp. 134-138.

Hornus, Jean-Michel. "L'American Board puis le Presbyterian Board en Syrie et au Liban: le Synode libano-syrien." *Proche-Orient Chrétien,* 1958, pp. 243-62; 1959, pp. 42-55 and 350-57; 1960, pp. 26-41 and 146-63; 1961, pp. 235-53 and 321-39.

──────. "L'American Board en Turquie et le developpement du Protestantisme arménien." *Proche-Orient Chrétien,* 1958, pp. 37-68 and 149-167.

──────. "Les origines de la mission jusqu'au partage entre les different sociétés." *Proche-Orient Chrétien,* 1957, pp. 139-51.

"Human Rights Review: The Situation of Christian Minorities in Turkey Since the Military Coup d'Etat of September 1980." Brussels: Churches Committee on Migrant Workers in Europe, June 1982.

Register, Ray C. "Christian Witness in the State of Israel Today." *International Bulletin of Missionary Research,* January 1983, pp. 16-18.

Villain, Maurice, S. M. "Reflections on the Christian Communities of the Near East in Communion with Rome." *Eastern Churches Quarterly,* Summer 1961, pp. 119-125; Autumn 1961, pp. 177-188.